ANN ARBOR DISTRICT LIBRARY

31621017176518

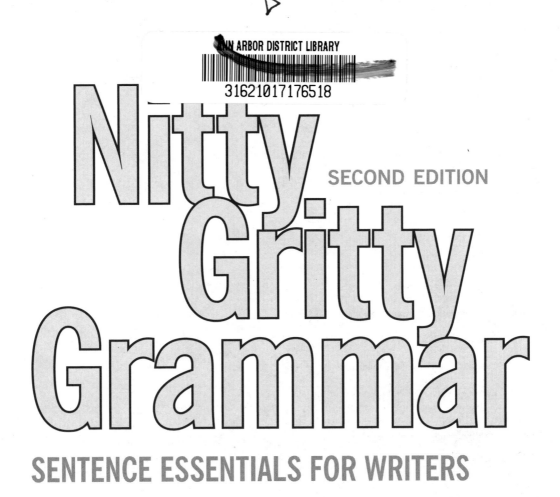

SECOND EDITION

Nitty Gritty Grammar

SENTENCE ESSENTIALS FOR WRITERS

TEACHER'S MANUAL

D1396650

A. Robert Young
Ann O. Strauch

CAMBRIDGE UNIVERSITY PRESS

Cambridge, New York, Melbourne, Madrid, Cape Town, Singapore, São Paulo, Delhi

Cambridge University Press
32 Avenue of the Americas, New York, NY 10013-2473, USA

www.cambridge.org
Information on this title: www.cambridge.org/9780521606554

© Cambridge University Press 2007

This publication is in copyright. Subject to statutory exception
and to the provisions of relevant collective licensing agreements,
no reproduction of any part may take place without the written
permission of Cambridge University Press.

First published by St. Martin's Press 1994
First edition © Cambridge University Press 1998
Second edition published 2007
2nd printing 2008

Printed in the United States of America

A catalog record for this book is available from the British Library.

ISBN-13   978-0-521-60654-7 Student's Book

ISBN-13   978-0-521-60655-4 Teacher's Manual

Cambridge University Press has no responsibility for the persistence or
accuracy of URLs for external or third-party Internet Web sites referred to in
this publication, and does not guarantee that any content on such Web sites is,
or will remain, accurate or appropriate.

Cover and book design: Adventure House, NYC
Text composition: Page Designs International

Cambridge University Press would like to thank Jane Sturtevant for her work on this book.

Contents

Introduction

INTRODUCTION TO *NITTY GRITTY GRAMMAR*

Nitty Gritty Grammar, Second Edition, is designed to help developing writers master the areas of English grammar that are common stumbling blocks for them, such as sentence fragments, incorrect article usage, and run-on sentences. The grammar is explored within the context of readings from many genres, including fiction by John Grisham and Roald Dahl, comic strips, and an excerpt from the 9/11 Commission Report. Inductive reasoning tasks, popular in the first edition, and thorough explanations provide support for all learners. Exercises, which range from controlled to open-ended, help students develop their understanding and confidence. Writing assignments throughout each chapter provide students with natural and stimulating contexts in which to use the grammar.

Although *Nitty Gritty Grammar* uses writing to teach grammar, it is a grammar book, not a composition course. Teachers may want to supplement the material in this book with a composition text. Also, it is not necessary to teach every chapter in order. Pick and choose based on students' needs.

ORGANIZATION OF THE STUDENT'S BOOK

The Student's Book is divided into 15 chapters, which are grouped into sections. Each chapter covers a broad grammar topic, which is broken down into subtopics, or parts. Each part presents a series of grammar points, or guidelines, that address form and usage. For example, *Chapter 5, Articles,* has two parts: Articles with Singular Count Nouns and Articles with Plural and Noncount Nouns. The Grammar Points under each part systematically explain the use of articles for each type of noun.

FEATURES OF THE TEACHER'S MANUAL

This Teacher's Manual provides the following support for teachers:

- Background information for the opening reading selections, which you may want to share with your students
- Common "trouble spots" for students and ways to handle them
- Additional information on the usage of the grammar
- Additional example sentences that illustrate the grammar and can be used to clarify or check students' understanding of the concepts
- Additional explanation of the practice exercises to help you understand their purpose and to prepare students for them
- Suggestions on how to develop, vary, or streamline the lessons for your class
- Answers to all exercises, except for those that appear in the Student's Book as part of the explanation and those that are answers to open-ended exercises

USING THE BOOK

Suggested below are "generic" approaches and techniques for each part of a chapter that can be used throughout the Student's Book. Other suggestions are included in the page-by-page notes.

Introduction to the Topic

This introduction gives you a brief description of the grammar topic that will be covered in the chapter. It does not need to be taught, but serves as a handy orientation for you and your students.

Refreshing Your Memory

Sometimes material in an earlier chapter is essential for students to have learned so that they can understand the current chapter. Refreshing Your Memory poses a few questions about this key grammar, providing a quick and focused review. If you are teaching the chapters out of sequence, these questions highlight the material you should review and may need to pre-teach. This feature also occurs in the Section Reviews.

Have students answer the questions in pairs or small groups. Then refer students to the Chapter Review of the chapter in which the grammar was presented and have them self-check their answers. Finally, review the answers as a class. If students seem unsure of their answers, review the grammar points that correspond to the problematic material.

Exploring the Topic

The grammar topic is presented in context in Exploring the Topic, usually in a literary passage. An identification task or a few inductive questions lead students to begin thinking about the grammar.

You may want to prepare students to read the passage by assessing their prior knowledge of its content or context ("You are going to read an excerpt from a novel about a private investigator. What do you know about private investigators?"). Give them any necessary background information (provided in this Teacher's Manual). This will ensure that students have the essential frame of reference in which to analyze the grammar.

Chapter Parts and Grammar Points

After the grammar topic is explored within the reading, it is divided up into subtopics, or parts. The guidelines for using each subtopic are systematically presented through a series of grammar points. Typically, these points are presented in three steps:

1) Exploring the Grammar Point This inductive exercise introduces the grammar point. It asks students to read example sentences and consider questions about form and/or meaning. Answers appear in this Teacher's Manual or in the Understanding the Grammar Point section that follows.

2) Understanding the Grammar Point This is a deductive exercise that answers the questions posed and presents a thorough explanation of the point. The exercise ends with a summary of the grammar point set in a blue "Nitty Gritty" box, which makes a handy reference tool as students work through the chapter.

This Teacher's Manual provides additional examples of the grammar point, which you may want to use to clarify the point or check students' understanding. If you wish, you may use these examples to present the grammar point with the Student's Books closed.

3) Practice Practice exercises follow most Grammar Points. When two Grammar Points contain intertwined ideas, one Practice exercise serves both points. The Practice exercises can be done in class as a group or as pair work, or they can be assigned as homework. Most exercises have set answers in the Teacher's Manual, although some exercises are open-ended. The answers are generally written using full forms rather than contractions to reflect the emphasis on academic writing. Here are some practical suggestions for giving students feedback on their answers:

For exercises with answers in the Teacher's Manual:

- Have students write the answers on the board, and go over them with the whole class. If you divide up the exercise and have three or four students writing side by side, it won't take long, and you can answer individual questions while they are writing.
- Share the answers with the class. Have students check their work individually at home or in class, where you can answer questions.
- Use an overhead projector or PowerPoint™ display to go over answers in class.

For open-ended exercises:

- Put students in groups to check each other's answers. Provide a clear time frame for this and make it clear that everyone in the group is responsible for every answer on every paper. (To reinforce this, tell students that after they check everyone's answers, you will have them trade papers and explain the answers on the paper they have to a partner in their group.) Afterwards, call on one student from each group to write his or her answer for one of the questions. Go over the answers on the board. Address your comments to the group, not the individual student.
- Have students check each other's answers in groups, as above. Then have them exchange papers with another group. Each group chooses an answer that they still believe is wrong, and writes it on the board. They then explain the mistake(s) they see and show how to correct it (them). The class decides if they are right or not.
- With both of these techniques, while students are discussing and correcting answers, move around the room looking at their work, pointing out but not correcting problems, and answering questions.

Writing Assignments

The writing assignments in *Nitty Gritty Grammar* are meant to stimulate students' thinking so that they feel motivated to write. Therefore, it is important that you first work on developing students' ideas. Then, once students are happy with their ideas, begin working on the grammar. Here are four suggestions for introducing the writing assignments:

- With historical topics or those that may be outside the realm of students' experiences, students might need some help thinking of things to write about. Examples would be *A historic incident from your country of origin*, Student's Book page 10, and *A road trip*, Student's Book page 144. Have students brainstorm ideas on the board. Write the list yourself or have two or three students write as others suggest ideas. Students might also brainstorm supporting ideas and interesting details for the most likely topics. For another approach, generate a list of questions with students to help focus them on the task (e.g., *What happened? When did it happen? Where did it happen? Who was there? Why is it important?*).

- With personal-history topics, have students discuss their stories with a partner. Examples would be *A disagreement,* Student's Book page 127, and *A special celebration,* Student's Book page 108. For topics such as *A disagreement,* you may want to brainstorm words that are associated with disagreements. As you list the words, categorize them by parts of speech. For *A special celebration,* discuss what makes a story interesting or entertaining (e.g., "I can see/hear/feel what is going on in the story because the writer uses descriptive words." "The writer shares how he feels or thinks."). Then decide together on a quick checklist listing the qualities of a good story for students to refer to as they write. After writing, partners can use the checklist to evaluate each other's work. This will ensure that criticism stays constructive.

- For opinion topics, students need to present compelling reasons for their opinions. Examples would be *When should a couple start a family?,* Student's Book page 26, and *Does everyone need a college education?,* Student's Book page 36. One way to help them prepare for this is to put them first in small groups with similar views and have them generate supporting ideas and persuasive arguments. Then put them in pairs or groups with opposing views and have them debate their ideas. Alternatively, you might prepare them with an informal debate in class.

- For imaginative topics, you might try a modified jigsaw approach. Examples would be *The purchase of Manhattan Island,* Student's Book page 9, and *Your rich relative,* Student's Book page 187. Put students in groups to develop a common story. They might choose a serious approach or a humorous one. After students have written the assignment individually, put them in pairs with students from other groups (who will have different stories), and have them read their stories to each other.

As students write, walk around and provide feedback on their ideas. Make a note of common weaknesses in grammar to address a bit later. You may also have students read their work to a partner for additional feedback. When students are happy with their ideas, begin to work on grammar. Now is the time to address the common weaknesses you noted previously. Then you may want to create with students a checklist of grammar points for them to use to edit their work. When students have finished editing, invite volunteers to read their work aloud. Discuss the strengths of the work in terms of its content. You may also want to point out appropriate use of grammar, as you see fit. Then have students read their work to each other.

Chapter Review

The list of Nitty Gritty guidelines is meant to provide a quick summary of the important points in the chapter and serve as a ready reference for students while they do the exercises. The information does not have to be taught again at this point.

The first Review Practice exercise is often a traditional short-answer or sentence-completion task that reminds students of key points and grammar terms from the chapter. It is best done in class in preparation for the other exercises. Most other Review Practice exercises are editing tasks in which students correct a variety of errors in a text. All Review Practice exercises have answers in this Teacher's Manual.

The techniques suggested above for correcting Practice exercises are also appropriate for Review Practice exercises.

Section Review

Section Reviews combine grammar points from two to four chapters for additional review, and exercises mix grammar points from all chapters. For this reason, the Section Review is not appropriate unless you have taught all the chapters in the section.

Each of the five Section Reviews begins with Refreshing Your Memory. This is somewhat different from exercises of the same name that begin some chapters. Here, the purpose is to bring to mind some of the principal teaching points from all the related chapters in the section. Refreshing Your Memory is best done in class before assigning the other exercises.

The rest of the exercises in the Section Review are editing exercises, and they all have answers in the Teacher's Manual. The techniques suggested above for correcting Practice exercises are also appropriate for Section Review Practice exercises.

Sentence Essentials

1

Parts 1 and 2 of this chapter teach about the features of subjects and verbs. If your students are familiar with the concepts of subjects and verbs, you may wish to skip Parts 1 and 2 or merely assign them for homework. Part 3 is a one-page review of sentence capitalization and end punctuation.

EXPLORING THE TOPIC

The passage "Flat or Round?" was written especially for *Nitty Gritty Grammar,* in the style of popular nonfiction writing. The questions that follow the passage focus students' attention on subjects and verbs.

Answers (Student's Book page 2)
1. Which subject is two words joined by *and*?   *Scholars and geographers*
2. Which verb is two words joined by *and*?   *Took . . . and sailed*

Grammar Point 1 ⟩ Noun Subjects

UNDERSTANDING THE GRAMMAR POINT
Additional examples with noun subjects (Student's Book page 2)
- **Olmsted and Vaux** designed New York's Central Park.
- **History** is destiny.
- **Listening to music** can be relaxing.

Practice 1.1
Answers (Student's Book page 3)
1. Variety is the spice of life.
2. Honesty is the best policy.
3. Still waters run deep.
4. A friend in need is a friend indeed.
5. Absence makes the heart grow fonder.
6. Two wrongs don't make a right.
7. Things are not always what they seem.
8. Actions speak louder than words.

UNDERSTANDING THE GRAMMAR POINT

Additional example (Student's Book page 3)

nouns   pronoun

Olmsted and **Vaux** designed New York's Central Park. **They** designed many other beautiful parks.

Practice 2.1

Answers (Student's Book page 4)

Harriet Tubman

N
1. Harriet Tubman was a slave in Maryland in the 19th century.

P
2. She escaped from her owner.

P
3. Later, she became the most famous "conductor" on the Underground Railroad.

P
4. She helped hundreds of other slaves escape to freedom.

N
5. The Underground Railroad was not an actual railroad.

P
6. It was a secret network of safe places called "railroad stations."

N
7. Escaping slaves traveled from station to station on their way to the North and freedom.

N
8. The conductors were free blacks and white abolitionists.

UNDERSTANDING THE GRAMMAR POINT

Additional examples (Student's Book page 4)
- **My sister and her husband** moved away two years ago.
- **She and I** don't see each other often.

Practice 3.1

Answers (Student's Book page 5)

Christopher Columbus

1. The king and queen of Spain paid part of the cost of the voyage.
2. The Santa María, Niña, and Pinta were Columbus's three ships.
3. Columbus and his 104 crewmen left Spain on August 3, 1492.
4. On October 8, ducks and other land birds flew near the ships.
5. On the island of Guanahaní, Taino men and women greeted Columbus.
6. Their peaceful manner and handsome appearance impressed him.

EXPLORING THE GRAMMAR POINT

Answers (Student's Book page 6)

(See Understanding the Grammar Point on Student's Book page 6 for explanations.)

• What does the word *it* mean in sentence 1?   *It means "the store."*
• What does *it* mean in sentence 3?   *It means something like "today."*
• Is *there* the subject of sentence 2?   *No, the subject is* they.
• In which sentence does *there* refer to a place?   *Sentence 2*

Additional examples

• **There's** a new theater in town. **It's** for plays and dance.
• We can't go **there** tonight, though.
• **It's** Monday, and they're closed on Mondays.

UNDERSTANDING THE GRAMMAR POINT

Additional examples (Student's Book page 6)

• **There's** a Greek play there now.
• Last month **there were** two dance companies performing there.

Practice 4.1

Answers (Student's Book page 7)

1. The time was 9:20. It was 9:20.
2. The day was Tuesday. It was Tuesday.
3. The date was November 2. It was November 2.
4. The weather in spring is cold and rainy. In spring, it is cold and rainy.
5. The distance from my home to my office is about thirty miles. It is about thirty miles from my home to my office.
6. The time necessary to go from my home to my office is about forty-five minutes. It takes about forty-five minutes to go from my home to my office.

Practice 4.2

Answers (Student's Book page 7)

1. After the party, ___there was___ a terrible mess in the living room.
2. ___There were___ dirty glasses on every table.
3. ___There were___ used napkins and leftover food everywhere, even on the floor.
4. ___There was___ an overturned soda bottle in one corner.
5. ___There were___ two broken chairs.
6. ___There was___ a stranger asleep on the sofa.

Answers (Student's Book page 7)

1. _____It_____ is mid-August.

2. _____It_____ is early in the morning.

3. ____There____ isn't a cloud in the sky.

4. _____It_____ is still cool.

5. ____There____ is dew on the grass.

6. ____There____ are only a few people in the park.

7. _____It_____ is a perfect day for a run.

8. ____There____ is just enough time for a run before class.

| Grammar Point 5 | **Verbs and Verb Phrases** |

UNDERSTANDING THE GRAMMAR POINT

Additional examples (one-word verbs) (Student's Book page 8)

- On my vacations, I always **go** somewhere.
- I **love** seeing new places.

Additional examples (verb phrases)

- I **am planning** a trip to South America next winter.
- I **was thinking** about Europe, but it's too expensive.
- I **have been** to Venezuela and Brazil.
- This time I **am going to visit** Bolivia and Peru.

Practice 5.1

Answers (Student's Book page 8)

Rapa Nui

Rapa Nui, or Easter Island, <u>is</u> 1400 miles from the nearest neighboring population. Polynesians <u>have lived</u> on the island for about 2500 years. The island <u>is</u> famous for its nearly 900 carved stone heads or *moai*. The tallest one <u>reaches</u> 70 feet. Many of them <u>were standing</u> when the first Europeans <u>arrived</u> in 1722. However, over the next hundred years, the islanders <u>pulled</u> them all down. Their descendants <u>say</u> the reason <u>was</u> anger and despair over the island's ecological and economic decline. Today, some moai <u>have been erected</u> again by archeologists. In addition to the famous moai, Rapa Nui <u>had</u> the only written language in Oceania. Today, very few examples of the writing <u>survive</u>, and scientists <u>are studying</u> them. So far, however, no one <u>has been able to read</u> them.

Grammar Point 6 ▶ Compound Verbs

EXPLORING THE GRAMMAR POINT

Answers (Student's Book page 9)

(See Understanding the Grammar Point for explanations.)

Each sentence has two verbs.

1. In the 17th century, Dutch traders <u>arrived</u> on Manhattan Island and <u>bought</u> it from some Native Americans for goods worth about $700 in today's money.
2. Unfortunately for the traders, those particular Native Americans <u>didn't live</u> on Manhattan and <u>didn't have</u> the right to sell the island.
3. They <u>accepted</u> the traders' goods and <u>went</u> on their way.

Additional examples

- Last summer, I <u>went</u> to Brazil and <u>studied</u> Portuguese.
- The school <u>emphasized</u> speaking and <u>arranged</u> for me to live with a Brazilian family.
- The family <u>welcomed</u> me and <u>helped</u> me a lot with my Portuguese.

Practice 6.1

Answers (Student's Book page 9)

The First Olympic Games

1. According to historic records, the Olympic Games began in 776 B.C. and occurred every four years until 393 A.D.
2. At their height, the Games lasted for five days and ended with a sacrifice of 100 oxen.
3. Athletes and officials walked to Olympus together and stopped on the way to make sacrifices.
4. The fighting events were very bloody and caused many deaths.
5. Olympic events honored the gods and tested skills needed in war.
6. Winners wore crowns of olive leaves and received special privileges in their home cities.

Grammar Point 7 ▶ Capital Letters and End Punctuation

UNDERSTANDING THE GRAMMAR POINT

Additional examples

- It's six o'clock.
- Are we ready to start?
- No, wait!

Practice 7.1

Answers (Student's Book page 10)

Flat or Round? (Part 2)

the story is false. why does every schoolchild in North America know it? did Columbus invent the story to make himself look good? there is no evidence that he did. this misconception is the fault of Washington Irving, a popular American writer of the 19th century. in his widely read book *The Life and Voyages of Christopher Columbus,* Irving told a long, detailed, and fascinating story about scholars' opposition to Columbus's theory and Columbus's heroic insistence that he was right. why did people believe Irving's story? at that time, more than three hundred years after the voyages, Columbus was a hero in this country. people wanted to believe the story was true. in fact, Irving simply made it up.

CHAPTER 1 REVIEW

Review Practice 1.1
Answers (Student's Book pages 11–12)

Three Exciting Days in Vancouver

1. Christine and Paul saw a lot on their vacation in Vancouver last summer.
2. They and their teenagers Molly and Charley spent three days in this interesting city.
3. On their first day, they flew into Vancouver International Airport and took the bus downtown.
4. Later that day, Paul and Molly explored the city on foot.
5. Christine and Charley took a bus to Simon Fraser University.
6. The next morning, the family got up early and took a taxi to Stanley Park.
7. At the park, Paul and the kids visited the aquarium.
8. Christine went to see the Indian ruins and met the family later at the zoo.
9. On the third day, the four of them rented a car and drove to a wilderness area outside of town for a picnic.
10. Later, they drove to the historic area of Vancouver and looked around in the stores.
11. That night, they all had dinner in Chinatown and finished their evening listening to jazz.
12. By the time they got home, Christine, Paul, and the kids were tired.

Review Practice 1.2
Answers (Student's Book page 13)

1. __Our classroom__ is fairly large.
2. __It__ has four large windows for light and air.
3. __There__ is a large desk for Ms. Ball's books and materials.
4. __Ms. Ball__ usually arrives a few minutes early.
5. __She__ takes attendance as soon as the bell rings.
6. __There__ is a whiteboard on the wall behind her desk.
7. __She__ often writes on the board to show us the important points.
8. __We / The students__ sit at smaller desks.
9. __There__ are twenty of them arranged in rows.
10. __We__ all sit down at the beginning of class.
11. __We__ often move around during class to work with classmates.
12. __The class / Our class__ is at night, on Mondays, Wednesdays, and Fridays.
13. __It__ is late when we get out.
14. __It__ is usually 10:00 P.M.

Review Practice 1.3

The information about Squanto and his life is true.

Answers (Student's Book page 14)

The Amazing Life of Squanto

Squanto was _____**born**_____ in 1580 in Patuxet, which is now Plymouth,
                    1

Massachusetts. At about the age of 25, he and _**four other Native American men**_ were
                                                              2

_____**captured**_____ and _____**taken**_____ to England. _____**He**_____
           3   4   5

_____**lived**_____ in England for nine years and _____**learned**_____ to speak
          6   7

English.

In 1614 _____**Squanto / he**_____ _____**returned**_____ to America. In the same year,
                    8   9

_____**he**_____ was _____**captured**_____ again and _____**taken**_____
        10   11   12

to Spain. There, _____**he**_____ was _____**sold**_____ as a slave and
                       13   14

_____**bought**_____ by Spanish friars, who freed him. _____**He**_____
         15   16

_____**lived**_____ with the friars for four years.
         17

In 1618, _____**Squanto / he**_____ traveled from Spain to England. Later the same year,
                    18

_____**Squanto / he**_____ and _**Captain Thomas Dermer**_ _____**sailed**_____ to
            19   20   21

America and _____**mapped**_____ the coast of New England.
                      22

In 1619, _____**Squanto / he**_____ _____**arrived**_____ home at Patuxet for
                    23   24

the second time and _____**found**_____ that all of his tribe had died of fever.
                             25

_____**He**_____ _____**went**_____ to live with another tribe nearby.
        26   27

In December of 1620, _**some English colonists**_ called Pilgrims _____**arrived**_____
                                  28   29

at Patuxet and _____**named**_____ it Plymouth. _____**They**_____
                         30   31

_____**did not have**_____ adequate food and shelter and _____**did not know**_____ how to
           32   33

hunt. That winter, _____**half**_____ of the Pilgrims _____**died**_____.
                           34   35

In the spring, _____Squanto_____ _____went_____ back to Patuxet
36   37

and _____lived_____ there with the Pilgrims. _____He_____
38   39

_____taught_____ them how to hunt and grow food. In November,
40

_____Squanto / he_____ and _____the Pilgrims_____ celebrated the first Thanksgiving in
41   42

Plymouth.

In 1622, at the age of 42, _____Squanto_____ _____caught_____ a fever
43   44

and _____died_____.
45

Simple, Compound, and Complex Sentences

2

EXPLORING THE TOPIC

The passage "Home, Sweet Home" is adapted from the first pages of *Danny: The Champion of the World. Danny* is the story of nine-year-old Danny, his father, and an illegal but entertaining project—to shoot pheasants belonging to a rich and arrogant landowner.

The author, Roald Dahl (British, 1916–1990), had an interesting life. He worked in East Africa, was a pilot in the British Royal Air Force, worked for military intelligence, married an actress, and wrote dozens of popular and successful books for both adults and children.

The questions draw students' attention to the fact that a variety of sentence structures (Version 1) is more interesting than a string of simple sentences (Version 2).

Answers (Student's Book pages 15–16)
- Do both versions give the same information?   *Yes*
- Which version is better? Why?   *Version 1 is better because the different sentence structures are more interesting, whereas in Version 2 they are all the same. Also, the sentences in Version 1 use words like* so, although, *and* because, *which show relationships among the ideas.*

Grammar Point 1 ▷ Clauses

EXPLORING THE GRAMMAR POINT

Additional examples (Student's Book page 16)
- we lived in an old gypsy trailer (clause)
- behind a gas station
- we did not have lights (clause)
- in the trailer
- especially in the evenings
- the kerosene lamp was turned low (clause)

UNDERSTANDING THE GRAMMAR POINT

Practice 1.1

Answers (Student's Book page 17)

_C_ 1. when I was four months old

_C_ 2. I had no brothers or sisters

_NC_ 3. a square brick building to the right of the office

_NC_ 4. was the workshop

_C_ 5. because the electricity people said it was unsafe

<u>C</u> 6. there was a wood-burning stove

<u>NC</u> 7. to keep us warm in the winter

<u>NC</u> 8. a kerosene lamp hanging from the ceiling

<u>C</u> 9. when I was in bed

<u>C</u> 10. my father was telling me stories

Grammar Point 2 — Independent Clauses

UNDERSTANDING THE GRAMMAR POINT

Additional examples (Student's Book page 17)

- Jenna is 26 years old.
- She works at a language learning center for children.
- The children are ages 4 to 10.
- This summer, some of the classes are free.

Practice 2.1

Answers (Student's Book page 17)

I am proud of my brother and sister. ^Tthey are taking classes at Bronx Community

College in New York. ^Tthey also work. ^Mmy sister works twenty hours a week. ^Mmy brother

works twenty-five hours a week. ^Iit is not easy to work and go to school at the same time.

Grammar Point 3 — Dependent vs. Independent Clauses

EXPLORING THE GRAMMAR POINT

Additional examples (Student's Book page 18)

- **Incorrect:** Roald Dahl worked in East Africa. When he was a young man.
  Correct: Roald Dahl worked in East Africa when he was a young man.

- **Incorrect:** Although he was British. His first story was published in the U.S.
  Correct: Although he was British, his first story was published in the U.S.

- **Incorrect:** If you like *Danny: The Champion of the World.* You might also like *Charlie and the Chocolate Factory.*
  Correct: If you like *Danny: The Champion of the World,* you might also like *Charlie and the Chocolate Factory.*

UNDERSTANDING THE GRAMMAR POINT

Practice 3.1

Answers (Student's Book page 19)

<u>D</u> 1. (when) I was four months old

<u>I</u> 2. my mother died suddenly

3. we lived in an old gypsy trailer behind a gas station

___D___ 4. (although) we had electric lights in the workshop

___I___ 5. we did not have them in the trailer

___D___ 6. (because) the electricity people said it was unsafe

___I___ 7. I loved it especially in the evenings

___D___ 8. (when) I was in bed

___I___ 9. my father was telling me stories

Grammar Point 4 ▶ **Simple Sentences**

EXPLORING THE GRAMMAR POINT

Answers (for the underlining task on Student's Book page 19)

1. Danny was four months old.

2. Danny and his father lived in an old gypsy trailer behind a gas station. (compound subject)

3. Danny's father repaired cars and looked after his son. (compound verb)

Additional examples

• My family lived in the woods.

• My father built a log cabin and drove an old truck.

• My sisters and I learned to read at home with my mother.

UNDERSTANDING THE GRAMMAR POINT

Practice 4.1

Grammar Point 5 identifies sentences 2, 3, and 8 as compound sentences.

Answers (Student's Book page 20)

_____simple_____ 1. There were five children in my family, three girls and two boys.

_____not_____ 2. My brother and I were the youngest, and we were identical twins.

_____not_____ 3. The family could recognize us, but no one else could.

_____simple_____ 4. My brother was good at math.

_____simple_____ 5. In high school, he sometimes went to my math classes and almost always took my tests for me.

_____simple_____ 6. They never caught us.

_____simple_____ 7. Now, in college, I am having a terrible time trying to pass my required math course.

_____not_____ 8. Unfortunately for me, my brother is going to a different college, so he can't help me.

EXPLORING THE GRAMMAR POINT

Additional examples (Student's Book page 20)

- My parents got visas in September 1998, and we arrived in Chicago in December.
- I liked the cold weather, but it was hard for my parents.
- My mother had to go to work, so she bought a big, down-filled coat.

UNDERSTANDING THE GRAMMAR POINT

Additional information

The coordinator *and* shows that the idea expressed by the second clause is an *addition* to the idea expressed by the first. *But* shows that the second clause is an *exception* to the first. *So* shows that the first clause is a *cause* and the second clause is an *effect*.

The idea of a logical relationship between two clauses in a sentence is reviewed in Practice 5.3.

Practice 5.1

Answers (Student's Book page 21)

A Child's Nest

Our parents were a blend of opposites. My mother was kind [1]*and* gentle. She had a far-seeing wisdom [2]*and* expected only the best from her fellow human beings. My father was a man with a high level of intelligence, ([3]*but*) he had a low level of tolerance. Patience was not one of his qualities. He loved trees, birds, [4]*and* all his farm animals. He appreciated nature, ([5]*but*) he viewed his fellow human beings with a suspicious eye. He never expected too much from them.

There were seven children in the family, ([6]*and*) we grew up free as birds. We were far away from the outside influence of the city, ([7]*so*) we grew up in a world of simplicity. Our farm was our world, ([8]*and*) nature was our teacher. We absorbed the natural order of things [9]*and* were free to grow up at our own pace in a quiet place close to the earth.

Practice 5.2

Answers (Student's Book page 22)

1. My father had a quick sense of humor, and the family loved his jokes.
2. He was smart and funny, but he was not a patient man.
3. My father had a degree from UCLA, but my mother did not finish college.

4. My mother valued education, so she took night classes.

5. My father always had a new car, and he washed it every Saturday.

6. My mother didn't like to drive, so my father did most of the driving.

Practice 5.3

Answers (Student's Book page 22)

_no_ 1. My mother is an attorney, and my sister is a teenager.

_OK_ 2. My mother is an attorney, and she's very good at her work.

_no_ 3. My sister is in the tenth grade, and she went to Sea World last year.

_OK_ 4. My sister is in the tenth grade, and she goes to Lincoln High School.

_OK_ 5. My sister is interested in marine animals, so she went to Sea World last year.

_OK_ 6. My brother raises chickens, but he won't eat any kind of meat.

_no_ 7. My brother plays the piano, but he won't eat any kind of meat.

_OK_ 8. My brother is a vegetarian, so he won't eat any kind of meat.

| Grammar Point 6 | **Longer Compound Sentences** |

Additional information (Student's Book page 23)

A long compound sentence may be grammatically correct, but difficult to read and understand. The writer should determine if a long compound sentence needs to be broken up into shorter sentences. This grammar point and Practice 6.1 begin to give students a feel for how and when to break up a longer compound sentence, and provide some practice in doing so.

UNDERSTANDING THE GRAMMAR POINT

Sentence 1 is clearly understandable, and 3 is clearly too long. Sentence 2 is understandable and would be fine in conversation. However, it is awkward as written discourse. It should be broken up into two sentences. Note that sentence 3 is used as the first item in Practice 6.1.

Additional examples

• In theory, my children come home for dinner every night, but they have a lot of activities after school.

• In theory, my children come home for dinner every night, but they have a lot of activities after school, so it doesn't always work out that way.

• In theory, my children come home for dinner every night, but they have a lot of activities after school, so it doesn't always work out that way, and sometimes we don't eat together all week, so it's hard for me to know what they're doing in school.

Additional information

You may want to remind students that, in academic writing, sentences should not begin with a coordinator. Students may use _Because of this_ instead of _So,_ and _However_ instead of _But_ (both followed by commas). _And_ can simply be omitted at the beginning of a sentence. _So_ and _But_ may also be omitted as long as the logical relationship is still clear (as in the last sentence in the suggested answer for item 3 in Practice 6.1, below).

Practice 6.1

There are various correct ways to break up these sentences, so students' answers will vary.

Suggested answers (Student's Book page 23)

1. My sister and I waited a long time, but no one came. Finally, I told her to leave, and she did. Then I left too.
2. My mother did not finish college, but she valued education. Because of this, she took night classes for six years. Last month, we all went to her graduation.
3. My brother is a vegetarian, so he won't eat any kind of meat. However, he raises chickens and sells them for meat. A lot of people think this is very funny.
4. One Saturday, as a joke, my twin brother and I went out with each other's girlfriend. Unfortunately, the girls figured it out. They were really mad, so they broke up with us. We felt bad about it. We promised never to do it again, but they wouldn't forgive us.

Grammar Point 7	Form of Complex Sentences

EXPLORING THE GRAMMAR POINT

Additional examples (Student's Book page 24)

- When John was in college, he worked nights and weekends to pay his tuition.
- He borrowed books from the library because he couldn't afford to buy them.
- After he graduated, he got a great job as a librarian at a local college.

UNDERSTANDING THE GRAMMAR POINT

Practice 7.1

Answers (Student's Book page 24)

1. When most people think of endangered species , they think of animals.
2. We sympathize with animals because they move and breathe and have families.
3. No one seems concerned when plants are endangered.
4. Plants are important because they convert the sun's energy into food.
5. When the leaves of trees in rain forests breathe , they send large amounts of oxygen into the air.
6. If we kill too many of our plants , animal life will cease.

UNDERSTANDING THE GRAMMAR POINT
Additional examples (Student's Book page 25)

COMMON SUBORDINATORS	
Time	**When** I came to the U.S., I was 15. **As soon as** I got here, I had to go to school.
Cause/Effect	**Since** I didn't speak English, everything was strange and difficult.
Condition	Kids shouldn't have to start school without English **unless** they have a lot of support.
Contrast	**Although** it was hard at the time, now I'm glad we came here.
Purpose	We came **so that** we could have a better life.

Practice 8.1

If students use all the words in the box as directed, there is only one right answer for each blank. Alternate correct answers are given for numbers 3 and 8. However, the first answer given for each is the one needed if all the words in the box are to be used.

Answers (Student's Book page 26)

Wedding Plans

Jack and I are going to get married ___right after___ [1] we finish college.

___If___ [2] Jack is able to finish his senior project in time, we will both graduate this year, and the wedding will be in June. We want to have children ___as soon as / when / if___ [3] we can, but we may have to wait a while ___so that___ [4] we can both work and make some money. We both have college loans to pay back, and we want to buy a house ___before___ [5] we start a family. Luckily, I have a great job lined up already ___because___ [6] my father wants me to join him in his business. He owns a big hardware store, and I have always liked working there, ___although___ [7] it may be different ___when / if___ [8] I am a manager instead of one of the workers. Anyway, ___unless___ [9] something goes wrong, we should be able to start a family in a couple of years.

Grammar Point 9　Compound-Complex Sentences

EXPLORING THE GRAMMAR POINT

Answers (Student's Book page 27)

1. My father was an elementary school teacher, (and) he liked his job, (even though) it was hard work (and) he never made much money.
2. (Although) my parents loved each other very much, their ideas were very different, (and) they argued (whenever) they disagreed.

Additional example (Student's Book page 27)

• My brother and his wife got married (before) they finished college, (so) it was hard for them to get their degrees, (and) it was hard on their marriage too.

UNDERSTANDING THE GRAMMAR POINT

Practice 9.1

Answers (Student's Book page 27)

1. I loved it especially in the evenings (when) I was in bed <u>and</u> my father was telling me stories.
2. (If) Jack is able to finish his senior project in time, we will both graduate this year, <u>and</u> the wedding will be in June.

   We want to have children (as soon as) we can, <u>but</u> we may have to wait a while (so that) we can both work and make some money. (*And* joins two parts of a compound verb, not two clauses.)

   We both have college loans to pay back, <u>and</u> we want to buy a house (before) we start a family.

   He owns a big hardware store, <u>and</u> I have always liked working there, (although) it may be different (when) I am a manager instead of one of the workers.

Grammar Point 10　A Common Mistake: Coordinator and Subordinator

Additional information (Student's Book page 28)

Unlike most grammar points in this book, this one addresses something students should *not* do. The most common subordinator + coordinator mistakes that students make are *although / even though / though + but*, and *because / since + so*.

EXPLORING THE GRAMMAR POINT

Answers (Student's Book page 28)

• Which correct sentence shows that the writer feels the two clauses are of equal importance?　*Sentence 1*
• Which shows that the independent clause is more important than the dependent clause?　*Sentence 2*

Additional examples

- **Correct:** I was good in school, so my brothers teased me.
- **Correct:** Since I was good in school, my brothers teased me.
- **Incorrect:** Since I was good in school, so my brothers teased me.

UNDERSTANDING THE GRAMMAR POINT

Practice 10.1

Grammatically, these sentences are correct with either the subordinator or the coordinator crossed out. The meanings are somewhat different. Both answers are given below.

Answers (Student's Book page 28)

1. ~~Because~~ my grandfather was very tall and had a long beard, so I thought he looked like God.
   Because my grandfather was very tall and had a long beard, ~~so~~ I thought he looked like God.

2. ~~Although~~ his beard was white, but I didn't think of Santa Claus.
   Although his beard was white, ~~but~~ I didn't think of Santa Claus.

3. ~~Since~~ I thought he looked like God, so I was afraid of him.
   Since I thought he looked like God, ~~so~~ I was afraid of him.

4. ~~Although~~ my parents tried to reason with me, but I refused to kiss him or sit on his lap.
   Although my parents tried to reason with me, ~~but~~ I refused to kiss him or sit on his lap.

5. ~~Because~~ my grandfather loved me dearly, so this must have hurt his feelings.
   Because my grandfather loved me dearly, ~~so~~ this must have hurt his feelings.

6. ~~Even though~~ I always cried when I saw my grandfather, but he was always kind to me.
   Even though I always cried when I saw my grandfather, ~~but~~ he was always kind to me.

7. Unfortunately, ~~since~~ I didn't see him very often, so I couldn't get used to him.
   Unfortunately, since I didn't see him very often, ~~so~~ I couldn't get used to him.

8. ~~Even though~~ I wasn't able to enjoy my grandfather's visits when I was small, but I came to love him when I was older.
   Even though I wasn't able to enjoy my grandfather's visits when I was small, ~~but~~ I came to love him when I was older.

Review Practice 2.1

Optional activity

Have students underline the subjects and verbs of clauses and circle the coordinators and subordinators in the passage below. This can be done before they add capital letters and periods, or after you have gone over the answers.

Answers (Student's Book pages 29–30)

The Day the Ground Fell Beneath My Feet

    M
my most frightening experience was a big earthquake in Japan. **A** at that time, I was

in the second grade. **M** my friend and I were about halfway home from school when the

earthquake occurred. **W** we were walking through a rice field. **M** my friend was whistling, and I

was trying to copy her tunes.

    A all of a sudden, the ground under my feet dropped about five inches. **A** at first, I was too

surprised to be scared. **A** as soon as I felt the earth again, my feet were taken to the right

and then jerked to the left. I staggered. **S** something struck my knee hard, but I couldn't feel

any pain.

    A after I fell to the ground, the shaking stopped. I stood up as fast as I could and hurried

home. **A** along the way, I came across a crying woman. **H** her knees were bleeding because

she had fallen into a ditch. **W** when I looked up at the sky, I noticed a dark gray cloud

floating heavily above me. **I** it gave me an uncanny feeling, and I almost began to cry.

    I in my city, many people got hurt. I can remember that bleeding woman and that gray

cloud clearly even now. **I** it was a very frightening experience, and I hope I never have to go

through anything like it again.

Review Practice 2.2

Optional activity

After going over the answers, have students identify the sentences as simple, compound, complex, or compound-complex. This could be done in several ways:

- Individually, in class, or for homework
- In pairs or groups, with each group responsible for a few sentences (there are 11), sharing and explaining their answers at the end
- In teams, as a game

Sentences in the answer key below are underlined for the optional activity. (Note that there are two simple sentences in the passage.)

Simple sentence

Compound sentence

Complex sentence

Compound-complex sentence

Answers (Student's Book page 30)

Bedtime Dolls

there were no dolls because these were the war years and such luxuries were non-existent. even though my little brother and I had no dolls, our resourceful mother gave us two little statues, one of Saint Theresa and the other of Baby Jesus. there was no shortage of statues in Irish homes at that time, so every night we took our much-loved statues to bed.

once a week my mother went to visit my grandmother a few miles down the road. if she was not home by our bedtime, my oldest sister Frances would put us to bed. this happened one winter's night, so Frances changed us into our night-clothes and led us upstairs to bed. just as we were falling asleep, I realized that we had no statues to keep us company. we knocked on the floor to call Frances, and when she appeared, we explained about our statues. she went in search of them, and as soon as she came back, she tucked the statues under the bedclothes beside us.

in the morning, instead of our two statues, we were cuddling two glass bottles. Frances had not been able to find the statues and had given us the bottles so that we would go to sleep.

Run-On Sentences and Sentence Fragments

REFRESHING YOUR MEMORY

Answers (Student's Book page 31)
1. What do all clauses have?   *A noun and a verb*
2. Which type of clause can stand alone as a sentence?   *An independent clause*
   Which type needs to be attached to another clause?   *A dependent clause*
3. What signals the beginning of a written sentence?   *A capital letter*
   What signals its end?   *In academic writing, almost always a period; in other writing, also a question mark or an exclamation point.*

EXPLORING THE TOPIC

The passage "Helping Nontraditional Students Succeed" was written for *Nitty Gritty Grammar* in a journalistic style. The task requires students to apply what they know about clauses in order to differentiate between correct and incorrect sentences (without yet naming them as run-on sentences or sentence fragments).

Answers (Student's Book page 31)
• Which version is better?   *Version 1*
• Why?   *The italicized parts of Version 1 are correct sentences (simple, compound, and complex). In Version 2, some of the italicized parts are written as sentences with capital letters and periods, but are not correct sentences.*

Explanation of the incorrect parts of Version 2
• The first italicized part (*They may get little support . . .*) has two independent clauses, but no coordinator.
• The second italicized part (*They need support . . .*) contains a dependent clause (beginning with *If*) written as a sentence.
• The third italicized part (*Colleges provide . . .*) has a dependent clause (beginning with *That*) written as a sentence. It also has an independent clause (beginning with *And*) that is not attached to another independent clause.
• The fourth italicized part (*They give them advisors . . .*) includes a group of words (beginning with *Providing*) that is not a clause, but is written as a sentence.

Grammar Point 1 ▸ Identifying Run-On Sentences

Note that Grammar Point 2 deals with correcting run-on sentences.

EXPLORING THE GRAMMAR POINT

Additional examples (Student's Book page 33)
* **Incorrect:** Many people choose a local college they may have different reasons for this.
* **Incorrect:** They may like their hometown, they may not have much money.
* **Incorrect:** They live with their parents they can save money.

UNDERSTANDING THE GRAMMAR POINT

Practice 1.1

Answers (Student's Book page 33)

A Crazy Day

Yesterday was a crazy <u>day I</u> was running around from early morning until late at night. My alarm clock went off at <u>6:00, I</u> jumped out of bed. I got dressed and ran out the door without having breakfast. I couldn't find a parking place on <u>campus I</u> parked eight blocks away. I ran to <u>class I</u> was late anyway. After my classes, I raced back to my <u>car, I</u> had to go to work at MacBuns. At work, the boss told me to work overtime. For the next nine hours, I fried hamburgers and unloaded delivery trucks. I got <u>home my</u> body ached all over. I was <u>disappointed, it</u> was too late to go swimming. I really needed a swim after running around all day.

Grammar Point 2 ▸ Correcting Run-On Sentences

UNDERSTANDING THE GRAMMAR POINT

Additional information (Student's Book pages 33–34)

1. Choose this option (two simple sentences) especially if
   * the independent clauses are not closely related, or
   * one of them is quite long.

2. Choose this option (a compound sentence) especially if
   * the two clauses are not too long, and
   * their relationship can be expressed with *but* or *so* (not just *and*).

3. Choose this option (a complex sentence) especially if
   * one clause is less important than the other, and
   * their relationship is well expressed by a subordinator.

Additional examples

Run-on sentence: Many people choose a local college they may have different reasons for this.

Two simple sentences: Many people choose a local college. They may have different reasons for this.

Run-on sentence: They may like their hometown, they may not have much money.

Compound sentence: They may like their hometown, or they may not have much money.

Run-on sentence: They live with their parents they can save money.

Complex sentence: If they live with their parents, they can save money.

Practice 2.1

Note that students should add commas before *but, so,* and *my body* and remove them before *because* in two places. Answers will vary.

Suggested answers (Student's Book page 33)

A Crazy Day

Yesterday was a crazy day. I was running around from early morning until late at night. My alarm clock went off at 6:00, *and* I jumped out of bed. I got dressed and ran out the door without having breakfast. I couldn't find a parking place on campus, *so* I parked eight blocks away. I ran to class, *but* I was late anyway. After my classes, I raced back to my car *because* I had to go to work at MacBuns. At work, the boss told me to work overtime. For the next nine hours, I fried hamburgers and unloaded delivery trucks. *When* I got home, my body ached all over. I was disappointed *because* it was too late to go swimming. I really needed a swim after running around all day.

Missing Subjects in Simple Sentences

EXPLORING THE GRAMMAR POINT

Additional examples (Student's Book page 34)

- **Incomplete:** Charles is taking four classes this semester. **In addition, has a job.**
- **Complete:** Charles is taking four classes this semester. **In addition, he has a job.**

UNDERSTANDING THE GRAMMAR POINT

Practice 3.1

Answers (Student's Book page 35)

Pele

Pele is one of the most famous soccer stars in history. _{He c}~~C~~ame from a poor family.

_{Pele / He w}~~W~~as born on October 23, 1940, in a small town in Brazil. All the people in the town

were poor. _{They d}~~D~~idn't have enough money to buy food every day. Of course, _{there}~~was~~ was not enough

money to buy a soccer ball. However, Pele's father was very inventive. _{He t}~~T~~ied some

old pieces of cloth together to form a ball. The young Pele and the other boys in the

neighborhood joyfully played soccer with this rag ball. _{They p}~~P~~layed barefoot every day until the

sun went down. Later, Pele played soccer on an organized team. Soon _{he} became the best

player on the team. Before Pele turned thirty, _{he} became a millionaire.

| Grammar Point 4 | **Missing Subjects in Dependent Adverbial Clauses** |

Adverbial clauses use subordinators, including those listed on page 25 of the Student's Book. The dependent clauses in *Chapter 2* are adverbial clauses.

EXPLORING THE GRAMMAR POINT

Additional examples

- **Incomplete:** **Although is hard for nontraditional students**, many of them manage to complete their degrees.

  Complete: **Although college is hard for nontraditional students**, many of them manage to complete their degrees.

- **Incomplete:** Some have husbands or wives who help them **so can succeed**.

  Complete: Some have husbands or wives who help them **so they can succeed**.

UNDERSTANDING THE GRAMMAR POINT

Practice 4.1

Answers (Student's Book page 37)

Thoughts of Dropping Out

Although I am fortunate to be in college full time, ^I^ sometimes feel like dropping out

of school for a while. If ^I^ weren't in college, I could have a real job and make some real

money. I think a lot of people are in college because ~~they~~ don't want to face real life, and ^I^

don't want to be one of those people. I know the time to work is after ^I^ finish college.

However, sometimes ^I^ just don't feel like waiting.

Grammar Point 5	**Missing Subjects in Dependent Adjective Clauses**

This grammar point teaches *that, who,* and *which* as subjects of adjective clauses. *Nitty Gritty Grammar* uses the term *adjective clause* rather than *relative clause* and does not use the term *relative pronoun* (using the pronouns themselves instead).

EXPLORING THE GRAMMAR POINT

Additional information (Student's Book page 37)

Judy Brady's satirical article "I Want a Wife" caused a sensation when it first appeared in 1972, and has been widely reprinted and quoted ever since. In it, she details the dozens of services that wives provide for their husbands, and ends by asking, "Who wouldn't want a wife?"

Additional examples
- I have good friends **who listen to me**.
- She's lucky to have a boss **that respects her opinion**.
- They want to buy a car **that never breaks down**.

UNDERSTANDING THE GRAMMAR POINT

Additional example (for Student's Book page 37)
- **Incomplete:** Judy Brady is a feminist has written many books and articles.
  Complete: Judy Brady is a feminist **who** has written many books and articles.

Additional examples (for the chart on Student's Book page 38)
- A green card is a document **that** allows an immigrant to live and work in the U.S. Immigrants **that** have green cards are allowed to leave the country and come back.
- People **who** come to this country on a student visa do not need a green card.
- The TOEFL test is an English test **which** many foreign students take.

Practice 5.1

There are two possible answers for each sentence.

Answers (Student's Book page 38)

1. The only American president ^{who}‸resigned from office was Richard Nixon.

2. Watergate was the incident ^{that / which}‸led to President Nixon's resignation.

3. Franklin Roosevelt is the only American president ^{that / who}‸served four terms.

4. The Peace Corps is an agency ^{that / which}‸sends American volunteers to work in foreign countries.

5. The person ^{that / who}‸initiated the first major action of the civil rights movement was Rosa Parks.

6. A draft is a system ^{that / which}‸registers young people for possible military service.

7. Bill Gates is an American businessman ^{that / who}‸became extremely successful.

8. Ralph Nader is a lawyer with an Arab background ^{that / who}‸was an early activist for consumer rights.

Grammar Point 6 | **Dependent Adverbial Clauses Standing Alone**

UNDERSTANDING THE GRAMMAR POINT

Additional examples (Student's Book page 39)

- Why didn't you call this morning?

  Because I forgot to recharge my cell phone.

- When are you coming home?

  As soon as I finish this report.

- Are you going to study tonight?

  If I don't get out of work too late.

Practice 6.1

Answers (Student's Book page 39) For answers to the second task, see **Suggested answers** on the following page.

__F__ 1. When I go on vacation.

__S__ 2. I like to have plenty of money.

__S__ 3. Nice hotels are expensive.

__S__ 4. When I stay in a cheap hotel, I don't feel comfortable.

__F__ 5. Because they are often on noisy streets.

__S__ 6. I don't sleep very well.

__F__ 7. When I don't sleep well.

__S__ 8. I can't enjoy daytime activities such as sightseeing and shopping.

__F__ 9. If you don't have plenty of money for your vacation.

S 10. Stay at home.

F 11. Until you save up enough for an enjoyable trip.

Suggested answers (for the second task on Student's Book page 39)

There is more than one way to correct some of the fragments. Students' answers may vary.

When I go on vacation, I like to have plenty of money. Nice hotels are expensive. When I stay in a cheap hotel, I don't feel comfortable. Because cheap hotels are often on noisy streets, I don't sleep very well. When I don't sleep well, I can't enjoy daytime activities such as sightseeing and shopping. If you don't have plenty of money for your vacation, stay at home until you save up enough for an enjoyable trip.

Practice 6.2

Answers (Student's Book page 40)

A Real Vacation?

My wife, Martha, is the Director of Admissions for a large university. She works very hard. In fact, she works too hard. Sometimes she works sixty hours a week. I want us to take a vacation ~~together. Because~~ *together because* we need some quality time alone, away from her job. Finally, I convinced Martha to go to Hawaii with me for a week. I made all the arrangements ahead of ~~time. Before~~ *time, before* she could change her mind. At first, Martha was reluctant to leave her work behind. After I arranged ~~everything. She~~ *everything, she* seemed happy with the plan. I didn't want her to do a ~~thing. Because~~ *thing because* I wanted this to be a real vacation for her. On the day we left, I even carried all her luggage down to the ~~taxi. Before~~ *taxi before* she had a chance to help. As she left the house, she carried only one little thing with her: her laptop computer.

Grammar Point 7 ▶ **Dependent Adjective Clauses Standing Alone**

EXPLORING THE GRAMMAR POINT

Additional information (Student's Book page 40)

The task draws on what students have already learned in Grammar Point 5 (to recognize dependent adjective clauses) and Grammar Point 6 (that a dependent clause cannot stand alone as a sentence). They should be able to infer that sentence 1 is correct and sentence 2 is incorrect.

Additional examples

• **Correct:** Some people have to work at jobs that they don't really like.
• **Incorrect:** Some people have to work at jobs. They don't really like.

UNDERSTANDING THE GRAMMAR POINT

Practice 7.1

Answers (Student's Book page 41)

1. In community colleges, there are many students who work more than 25 hours a week.
2. I have a few classmates who don't work at all.
3. Sachiko has a student loan that covers all her tuition.
4. Our college has a financial aid office, which helps students apply for scholarships.
5. Rafael should go and see a financial aid advisor who can help him apply for a scholarship.

Practice 7.2

Answers (Student's Book page 41)

1. I have a calculus class that I really like.
2. Akbar has a class that requires an essay every week.
3. Manzar bought a chemistry book that cost $95.
4. Adrian wrote a lab report that took three hours.
5. Marisela wrote a term paper that required library research.

Grammar Point 8 ▶ Added-Detail Fragments

This grammar point discusses sentence fragments that do not have a subject and / or a verb. Because such fragments often occur when student writers are adding details to their writing, *Nitty Gritty Grammar* refers to them as *added-detail fragments*.

EXPLORING THE GRAMMAR POINT

Additional examples (Student's Book page 42)

- **Incomplete:** I'm so tired. **Getting ready for a long trip.**
  Complete: I'm so tired getting ready for a long trip.
- **Incomplete:** Marc has a long workday. **Especially on Tuesdays and Thursdays.**
  Complete: Marc has a long workday, especially on Tuesdays and Thursdays.
- **Incomplete:** Kara is overbooked. **Working full time, taking care of her family, and going to school evenings and Saturdays.**
  Complete: Kara is overbooked. She works full time, takes care of her family, and goes to school evenings and Saturdays.
- **Incomplete:** I'm busy on weekends. **For example, cleaning the house, doing the laundry and the shopping, and also spending some time with my family.**
  Complete: I'm busy on weekends. For example, I have to clean the house, do the laundry and shopping, and also spend some time with my family.

Practice 8.1

This practice requires students to identify added-detail fragments. Practice 8.2 is a continuation of this practice, requiring correction of the fragments.

Answers (Student's Book page 43)

Muhammad Ali

Muhammad Ali was born Cassius Clay on January 17, 1942. <u>In Louisville, Kentucky.</u> The young Cassius showed an early interest in boxing. <u>For example, by taking boxing lessons when he was twelve years old.</u> In 1960, Clay won a gold medal in boxing at the Olympics in Rome. This success launched him on a career in professional boxing. In 1964, Clay became the world champion heavyweight boxer. <u>Beating Sonny Liston in the sixth round of their fight.</u> Then, in a rematch, he beat Liston again. <u>This time by a knockout in the first round.</u> Soon afterwards, Clay became a Muslim. <u>And changed his name to Muhammad Ali.</u>

Practice 8.2

The two versions of the paragraph below show the two different ways of correcting added-detail fragments. The best paragraph would use some of each kind of correction.

Answers (Student's Book page 43; attaching fragments to complete sentences)

Muhammad Ali

Muhammad Ali was born Cassius Clay on January 17, ~~1942. In~~ [1942, in] Louisville, Kentucky.

The young Cassius showed an early interest in boxing~~. For example~~ by taking boxing

lessons when he was twelve years old. In 1960, Clay won a gold medal in boxing at

the Olympics in Rome. This success launched him on a career in professional boxing.

In 1964, Clay became the world champion heavyweight ~~boxer. Beating~~ [boxer, beating] Sonny Liston in

the sixth round of their fight. Then, in a rematch, he beat Liston ~~again. This~~ [again, this] time by a

knockout in the first round. Soon afterwards, Clay became a ~~Muslim. And~~ [Muslim and] changed his

name to Muhammad Ali.

Muhammad Ali

Muhammad Ali was born Cassius Clay on January 17, 1942. ~~In~~ *He was born in* Louisville, Kentucky.

The young Cassius showed an early interest in boxing. For example, ~~by taking~~ *he took* boxing

lessons when he was twelve years old. In 1960, Clay won a gold medal in boxing at

the Olympics in Rome. This success launched him on a career in professional boxing.

In 1964, Clay became the world champion heavyweight boxer. ~~Beating~~ *He beat* Sonny Liston in

the sixth round of their fight. Then, in a rematch, he beat Liston again. This time *he won* by a

knockout in the first round. Soon afterwards, Clay became a Muslim. ~~And~~ *He also / At the same time, he* changed his

name to Muhammad Ali.

Review Practice 3.1

There is more than one way to correct some of the run-on sentences and sentence fragments in this review practice. Students' answers will vary.

Suggested answers (Student's Book page 44)

My First Day of College

My first day of classes at Miami Dade Community College was a disaster. Everything

was ~~fine. Until~~ *fine until* I got to the campus. The parking lot on Twenty-Seventh Avenue was

~~full there~~ *full, so there* was no place for me to park. Since I wanted to be on ~~time. I~~ *time, I* panicked and

parked in a staff ~~space. Near~~ *space near* the Administration Building. As I ran toward my English

class, I looked back and saw the campus ~~police. Giving~~ *police giving* me a ticket. Next, I discovered

that I didn't have my class schedule with ~~me, I~~ *me, and I* didn't remember the room number. The

schedule was in my ~~car there~~ *car, and there* were only a few seconds before the class was supposed

to start. In a greater panic, I ran back to the ~~car. As~~ *car as* fast as I could. When I reached

into my pocket for my keys, they were not there. They were in the ~~car. Which~~ *car, which* was

locked! As a result, I missed my first class. In the future, I plan to get to ~~school. With~~ *school with*

plenty of time to spare.

Review Practice 3.2

There is more than one way to correct some of the run-on sentences and sentence fragments in this review practice. Students' answers will vary.

Suggested answers (Student's Book page 45)

A Folk Tale: The Tiger's Whisker

Yun Ok was unhappy in her ~~marriage. Because~~ **marriage because** her husband did not treat her with

consideration. He didn't pay attention to her. When he spoke to ~~her. He~~ **her, he** was impolite.

Yun Ok became so unhappy that she decided to consult a famous wise man ~~had helped~~ **who had helped**

many ~~people. For example, marital problems~~ **people, for example, people with marital problems** and other types of family problems.

~~The unhappy~~ **When the unhappy** young woman explained her situation to the old man, he thought very

~~carefully. And~~ **carefully and** then answered. The old man told Yun Ok that he could solve her ~~problem.~~ **problem if**

~~If~~ she first brought him the whisker of a living tiger. Yun Ok trembled with ~~fear. After~~ **fear, but after** a few

minutes she agreed to do as he asked.

That night, Yun Ok went out to the mountainside to the cave of a ferocious ~~tiger. lived~~ **tiger that lived**

there. She took food with ~~her. That~~ **her that** a tiger would like. She put the food at the entrance

to the cave. Then she waited at a ~~distance. While~~ **distance while** the tiger ate. For several months, Yun

Ok brought food for the ~~tiger, gradually~~ **tiger, and gradually** the tiger got used to Yun Ok. Little by little, she

moved closer to the tiger ~~until could~~ **until she could** almost touch the beast. Finally, Yun Ok asked the

tiger for one of his ~~whiskers, he~~ **whiskers, and he** agreed.

As fast as she could, Yun Ok raced back to see the old man. In her hand, she held the

tiger's ~~whisker. The~~ **whisker, the** cure for her unhappiness. ~~Yun Ok~~ **When Yun Ok** handed the precious whisker to the

old man, he immediately tossed it into the fire.

"What are you doing?" she cried. "You've thrown away my last hope!"

"No," answered the old man. "If you know how to tame a vicious tiger, ~~surely can~~ **surely you can** do

the same with your husband."

Yun Ok returned home ~~slowly. Thinking~~ **slowly, thinking** about the old man's advice.

Review Practice 3.3

There is more than one way to correct some of the run-on sentences and sentence fragments in this review practice. Students' answers will vary.

Suggested answers (Student's Book page 46)

Fighting Procrastination

One of the most common time management problems is procrastination. ~~Means~~ [Procrastination means] not doing something until the last ~~minute. Or~~ [minute, or] until it is actually too late. For example, ~~writing a research paper. A~~ [a] student may not ~~begin~~ [begin writing a research paper] until the night before the assignment is ~~due.~~ [due,] ~~When~~ [when there] is not enough time to finish.

Getting started is the most difficult step for procrastinators. Let's suppose that you are procrastinating about doing a writing assignment. Break the assignment down into parts or ~~steps this~~ [steps. This] makes the task more manageable. Even if you work on it only twenty minutes a ~~day. Will~~ [day, you will] make some progress.

Here are some tips for beating procrastination:

1. Start ~~immediately. Before start~~ [immediately, before you start] thinking of reasons to delay. Once you ~~start, is~~ [start, it is] easier to keep going.

2. Don't try to be ~~perfect, can~~ [perfect. You can] always make revisions ~~later. If~~ [later if] you need to. In fact, all good writers revise their material.

3. Guard against temptations to ~~escape. Aren't~~ [escape. You aren't] really hungry and don't really need to make that phone call right now.

4. Work with another person. For example, if you're brainstorming ~~ideas. Do~~ [ideas, do] it with a classmate. This will help you keep working, and you may even get some ~~ideas will~~ [ideas that will] improve your writing.

SECTION 1 REVIEW

REFRESHING YOUR MEMORY

Answers (Student's Book page 47)

1. I arrived in the United States and met my first American on February 8, 2001.

    What is the verb of this sentence? *Arrived and met*
    What kind of verb is it? *It is a compound verb.*

2. It was very cold that day.

    What is the subject of this sentence? *It*
    What kind of subject is it? *A filler subject*
    What does it mean in this sentence? *The weather*

3. I had a sweater, but I didn't have a winter coat because I came from Belize.

    How many clauses does this sentence have? *Three*
    Are they independent or dependent clauses? *The first two are independent, the third is dependent.*
    What kind of sentence is it: simple, compound, complex, or compound-complex? *Compound-complex*

4. *An American woman. Who was standing next to me.* She noticed that I was cold.

    The two sentences *in italics* are incorrect. Why? *The first sentence is a subject without a verb – a sentence fragment. The second sentence has neither a subject nor a verb. It is an added-detail fragment.*
    How can you correct them? *There are two ways to correct them:*
    (1) An American woman who was standing next to me noticed that I was cold.
    (2) An American woman was standing next to me. She noticed that I was cold.

5. She had a winter coat and a ski jacket in her luggage, she lent me the ski jacket.

    This sentence is incorrect. Why? *It is two independent clauses joined by a comma – a run-on sentence.*
    How can you correct it? *There are two ways to correct it:*
    (1) She had a winter coat and a ski jacket in her luggage. She lent me the ski jacket.
    (2) She had a winter coat and a ski jacket in her luggage, so / and she lent me the ski jacket.

Section Review Practice 1.1

There is more than one way to correct some of the mistakes. Answers will vary.

Suggested answers (Student's Book pages 47–48)

My Pet Peeves

Two common annoyances in everyday ~~life. They really~~ <u>life really</u> bother me. The first one is the loudness of TV ~~commercials, television~~ <u>commercials. Television</u> has a lot of ~~commercials. Understand~~ <u>commercials, and I understand</u> that TV companies need many sponsors. That's OK, <u>but</u> I don't understand why the volume is so high. It hurts my ears. Sometimes I grab the remote control in a ~~hurry. And~~ **hurry and** turn the

volume ~~down. But~~ **down, but** this is a big ~~bother. Is~~ **bother. It is** stressful to me to hear the loud ~~commercials, is~~ **commercials, and it is**

annoying to have to turn the volume down and up again so often.

    The other annoyance is the large amount of junk mail ~~that receive~~ **that I receive**. My mailbox is

completely filled every ~~day. With~~ **day with** mostly useless material. I hate to sort through all the

junk to separate out what is important from what is not. Some junk mail pretends that

it is very important or ~~official. Is~~ **official. This is** very confusing and ~~time-consuming. For~~ **time-consuming for** a person like

~~me. Who~~ **me, who** cannot read English well. ~~I sure~~ **I am sure** that other people feel the way I ~~do, I sure~~ **do. I am sure** that

many ~~people tired~~ **people are tired** of advertisers intruding on their personal ~~lives. And~~ **lives and** robbing them of

their time and energy.

Section Review Practice 1.2

There is more than one way to correct some of the mistakes. Answers will vary.

Suggested answers (Student's Book page 48)

Not Such a Good Day

    When I came here to ~~California. I~~ **California, I** bought a new car right ~~away, even~~ **away. Even** though I had an

international driver's license, ~~but~~ I had never driven in this country. One day, I drove my

parents, my daughter, and my son to go shopping at Del Amo. We bought some things,

ate pizza, drank coffee, and talked with each ~~other, it~~ **other. It** was a good day.

    When we came out, I had to wait to turn ~~left. From~~ **left from** the parking lot. The cars were

going by very close to the front of my car. I thought maybe I was in the ~~way, I~~ **way, so I** backed ~~up.~~ **up**

~~Without~~ **without** looking in the rearview mirror. I backed into the car in back of ~~me. A~~ **me. It was a** new BMW.

    Oh, my God! I was so embarrassed. I didn't know what to ~~do, it~~ **do. It** was definitely my

fault. I showed the other driver my insurance ~~papers that~~ **papers. That** was all I could do. A good day

was changed to a bad ~~day, after~~ **day. After** that day, I drove more ~~carefully since~~ **carefully, and since** that day, I always

check the rearview ~~mirror. While~~ **mirror while** driving.

There is more than one way to correct some of the mistakes. Answers will vary.

Suggested answers (Student's Book page 49)

I Miss Peru

There are three things that I really miss about my country, ~~Peru. The~~ [*Peru. They are the*] food, my friends, and my family.

Peruvian dishes are made with special ~~seasonings, they~~ [*seasonings, so they*] have flavors that only Peruvian people know how to make. I really miss all the ~~ingredients. That~~ [*ingredients that*] I used to use to make my favorite ~~dishes. For~~ [*dishes, for*] example, the traditional dish called ~~cuy frito. Means~~ [*cuy frito, which means*] "fried guinea pig." ~~Is~~ [*It is*] made with a special sauce and served with rice, potatoes, and Peruvian salad. In this country, guinea pigs are pets. ~~Are~~ [*There are*] no guinea pigs in the supermarket.

Another thing I miss about my country is my ~~friends, we~~ [*friends. We*] used to enjoy going to each other's houses and spending time talking and joking around together. Also, we often used to go camping at the ~~river, was~~ [*river, which was*] a special ~~place, the~~ [*place. The*] air smelled of ~~flowers and~~ [*flowers, and*] the fresh air and quiet made us feel very ~~free, and~~ [*free. In fact,*] we really were free there because no one was watching us or telling us what to do.

The thing I miss most is my ~~family, miss~~ [*family. I miss*] my parents a lot, even though I have a family ~~here, but~~ [*here. I*] always remember their advice about life. ~~Before came~~ [*Before I came*] to this ~~country. My~~ [*country, my*] father told me, "If you believe great things will happen, anything is possible." I know now what he meant by that. I also miss fighting with my sisters, because we always made up and treated each other with a lot of affection afterwards . . . usually.

These are the things I miss the ~~most. When~~ [*most when*] I think about Peru. I hope in the future I can visit my country and experience all these dear things again.

Section Review Practice 1.4

There is more than one way to correct some of the mistakes. Answers will vary.

Suggested answers (Student's Book page 50)

The Joys of Camping

Camping is my ~~hobby, I~~ do it for ~~fun, have~~ found helpful results from it. First, ~~gives~~
> hobby. I   fun, but I have   camping gives

me the experience of working together with others. The spirit of teamwork should

be developed more than selfishness. In ~~camping are~~ many opportunities to work in
> camping there are

cooperation with others. Second, it cannot be denied that camping is an occasion to live

with many kinds of ~~people, therefore is~~ a good chance to practice suitable behavior with
> people. Therefore it is

~~others, to~~ know how others see me. Humanity is a mystery to ~~me, I~~ want to learn more
> others and to   me, so I

about myself and other people. That is my point of view in life. One more good result is

making many new friends. Camping has done this for me. When I join in working with

~~people. They~~ see that I am interested in ~~them. They~~ often become friends. Someone once
> people, they   them, and they

told me that he never wastes a chance to find another half of ~~himself, I~~ have found many
> himself, and I

new halves of ~~me. By~~ camping. Life is ~~boring. If~~ we have no hobbies or activities at ~~all,~~
> me by   boring if   all.

~~each~~ person has his or her own ~~choice, my~~ choice is camping.
> Each   choice, and my

Nouns

EXPLORING THE TOPIC

The passages are excerpted from *The First Deadly Sin* by Lawrence Sanders, published in 1973. In 1980 it was made into a movie starring Frank Sinatra, Faye Dunaway, and David Dukes. Lawrence Sanders was a journalist who published his first novel at the age of 50. When he died in 1998, he had published 37 novels.

The first task shows students some of the meanings that nouns can have. All the nouns in Part 1 are in italics. The second task requires students to recognize nouns in context.

Note that just as *bathroom* is a noun modifying *door* in Part 1, in Part 2, *dairy* is a noun modifying *products, lemon* is a noun modifying *juice,* and *hip* is a noun modifying *bones.* Nouns as modifiers are discussed in Grammar Point 2.

Answers (Student's Book page 52)

1. People: man, Daniel Blank, wife

   Places: high school, college, inside, bathroom

   Things: body, shoulders, thighs, inventory, mirror, door

   Concepts: separation, feet, activities, deterioration

   Activities: swimming, track, tennis

2.

   ### Daniel Blank (Part 2)

   He at once began a strict <u>program</u> of <u>diet</u> and <u>exercise</u>. He bought several <u>books</u> on <u>nutrition</u> and <u>systems</u> of physical <u>training</u>. He tried to avoid <u>starch</u>, <u>sugar</u>, <u>dairy</u> products, <u>eggs</u>, and red <u>meat</u>. He ate fresh <u>fruit</u>, <u>vegetables</u>, broiled <u>fish</u>, and <u>salads</u> with a <u>dressing</u> of fresh <u>lemon</u> <u>juice</u>. Within three <u>months</u>, he had lost twenty <u>pounds</u> and his <u>ribs</u> and <u>hip</u> <u>bones</u> showed.

Chart: Some Count Nouns

The chart displays some count nouns in both their singular and plural forms. This is basic information that will be useful in Part 1 of this chapter. The first two nouns in the chart are irregular in their plural forms, and the rest are regular. Students will work with singular nouns in Grammar Points 1 and 2, and with plural nouns in Grammar Points 3, 4, and 5, including irregular plurals in Grammar Point 5.

Optional activities

Have students write sentences with the singular and plural forms in the chart. Have two or three students work at the board and correct their sentences with the whole class. You might also elicit more singular nouns from students and invite them to supply the plural forms, or supply them yourself. (Someone may suggest a noncount noun. Noncount nouns are discussed in Part 2 of this chapter.)

Singular Count Nouns and Determiners

EXPLORING THE GRAMMAR POINT

Additional examples (from "A Child's Nest" on Student's Book page 21)

Version 1

Our parents were a blend of opposites. My mother was kind and gentle. She had a far-seeing wisdom and expected only the best from her fellow human beings. . . .

Version 2

Parents were blend of opposites. Mother was kind and gentle. She had far-seeing wisdom and expected only best from fellow human beings. . . .

Grammar Point 2 **Modifiers**

EXPLORING THE GRAMMAR POINT

Answer (Student's Book page 54)

Of course, this is a play on the word *possessive*. A possessive person can be difficult in a relationship. A possessive adjective (my, your, his, her, our, their) is just a part of speech.

UNDERSTANDING THE GRAMMAR POINT

In the cartoon, the word *possessive* is an adjective modifying the noun *adjective*. It goes between the article and the noun.

Practice 2.1

This practice requires students to recognize singular nouns, modifiers, and determiners. There are plural and noncount nouns in the passage as well as singular ones. If you feel that identifying the singular nouns may be too challenging for your students, you might list them on the board for reference while students underline their modifiers and determiners. (Plural nouns are discussed in Grammar Points 3, 4, and 5; noncount nouns are discussed in Grammar Points 6 and 7. Note that Grammar Point 3 works with plural nouns in this same passage.)

Answers (Student's Book page 55)

Choosing an Exercise Program

Before you begin an exercise program, you should identify your most important needs and choose a plan to meet them. Every plan has its own strengths. One program may be ideal for losing weight, while another program is better for building strength. This plan will give you defined muscles, while that plan will strengthen your cardiovascular system. Your best friend's program may work well for him or her, but it may not be the best plan for you.

An appropriate exercise program also has to fit your schedule. Julia's days were very full. She had two young children at home, and she was taking college courses at night. Even so, she wanted to add some fitness activities to her schedule. She found that she could do a twenty-minute exercise video while the kids were taking their naps.

Notes on the answers

- *Your best friend's program*   There are two singular nouns here. *Your best friend's* is a noun phrase consisting of a determiner + a modifier (adjective) + a singular possessive noun. The whole noun phrase modifies *program*.
- *at home, at night*   The singular nouns in these set phrases do not take determiners. See *Chapter 5,* Grammar Point 7, Student's Book page 76, for a list of such phrases.
- *a twenty-minute exercise video*   *Twenty-minute* is an adjective. Numerical noun adjectives are discussed in *Chapter 15,* Grammar Point 6, Student's Book page 253.
- *college courses*   *College* is a singular noun modifying a plural noun.

Grammar Point 3 ▶ Plural Nouns and Determiners

This grammar point contrasts plural nouns with singular nouns in their need for determiners.

EXPLORING THE GRAMMAR POINT

The answers to the task and the first question are given below. The second question is answered in the Student's Book in Understanding the Grammar Point.

Answers (to the underlining task on Student's Book page 55)

Choosing an Exercise Program

Before you begin an exercise program, you should identify your most important needs and choose a plan to meet them. Every plan has its own strengths. One program may be ideal for losing weight, while another program is better for building strength. This plan will give you defined muscles, while that plan will strengthen your cardiovascular system. Your best friend's program may work well for him or her, but it may not be the best plan for you.

An appropriate exercise program also has to fit your schedule. Julia's days were very full. She had two young children at home, and she was taking college courses at night. Even so, she wanted to add some fitness activities to her schedule. She found that she could do a twenty-minute exercise video while the kids were taking their naps.

Answers (to the questions on Student's Book page 55)

What determiners did you find?   *your, its, Julia's, some, the, their*

Which plural nouns do not have determiners?   *muscles, courses*

UNDERSTANDING THE GRAMMAR POINT

You might want to elicit additional examples for the chart.

Additional examples (Student's Book page 56)

Articles	(there are no others)
Possessive adjectives	his, its, our, their
Possessive nouns	North America's, the school's . . .
Plural demonstrative adjectives	(there are no others)
Plural quantity words	many, most . . .
The numbers *two* and higher	five, six . . .

Practice 3.1

The use of *the* is discussed in detail in *Chapter 5*, but students should be able to do this task without having studied that chapter.

Answers (Student's Book page 56)

Working It Out

~~People~~ listen to music while they exercise, although <u>people</u> watch TV. For me, best
<u>Some p</u> ^   <u>other</u> ^   <u>my</u> ^

<u>ideas</u> come while I'm working out. I'm a writer, and I often get stuck with my writing. I

find that if I wait, <u>ideas</u> will come. But they come faster when I'm exercising. When I'm

really stuck, I spend <u>hours and hours</u> walking, running, and lifting <u>weights</u>. ~~Hours~~ help
                                                                          <u>These h</u> ^

my writing and do <u>wonders</u> for my body. ~~Results~~ are welcome.
                                           <u>Both r</u> ^

Grammar Point 4 | **Forming Regular Plural Nouns**

Note that the guidelines in this discussion are for written forms, not pronunciation.

UNDERSTANDING THE GRAMMAR POINT

Be aware that not all languages mark nouns (for example, by adding -*s*) to show plurality. Languages such as Chinese, Korean, and Vietnamese do not make this distinction. Therefore, it is grammatically correct in those languages to say "I have two sister." You may want to spend more time explaining and practicing this point with speakers of those languages.

Additional examples (Student's Book page 57)

Chart 1: mother, walk, gift, day, massage

Chart 2: glass, rash, touch, box

Chart 3: party, baby

Chart 4: wife

Practice 4.1

Students should refer to the charts on page 57 while doing the exercise. You might want to have them work in pairs. (Note that *children* is an irregular plural. Irregular plurals are discussed in Grammar Point 5.)

Answers (Student's Book page 58)

Special Gifts

No elaborate ~~pastrys~~ *pastries*, no ~~boxs and boxs~~ *boxes and boxes* of gifts—my two brothers decided to give

their wives something special for their birthdays this year. Both of their ~~wifes~~ *wives* have two

small children. The kids are not ~~babys~~ *babies*, but they don't go to school yet either, and their

~~motheres~~ *mothers* are tired all the time. My brothers gave the two women six days at a spa

in Arizona.

It's a wonderful place. The rooms are decorated in shades of white with ~~touchs~~ *touches* of

blue. There are gift baskets of beauty ~~supplys~~ *supplies* in each room. The days are spent eating

delicious and healthy breakfasts, ~~lunchs~~ *lunches*, and dinners, getting gentle massages, taking

~~classs~~ *classes* in yoga, going on long walks, relaxing in the hot tubs, and not much else. My

sisters-in-law loved their ~~giftes~~ *gifts* and dream of going back again someday.

Grammar Point 5 | **Forming Irregular Plural Nouns**

UNDERSTANDING THE GRAMMAR POINT

Alternate presentation (books closed)

- Introduce the idea of irregular plural nouns: They do not end in -*s*.
- Choose a few regular and irregular nouns and list their singular forms on the board in random order. Choose nouns of which your students are likely to know the plural forms.
- Elicit the plural forms and write them next to the singular forms.
- Have volunteers go to the board and circle the pairs of irregular nouns.
- Point out that some irregular plurals (such as *fish*) have the same form as the singular noun.

Suggested examples (Student's Book page 59)

Singular	Plural
pencil	pencils
man	men
child	children
teacher	teachers
foot	feet
book	books
fish	fish

Practice 5.1

This practice focuses on one irregular noun, *person / people*. This is particularly useful for speakers of languages (Spanish is one) that use a noncount or singular form where English uses the plural *people*. If this is not an issue for your students, you may want to skip this practice.

Answers (Student's Book page 59)

1. _____**People**_____ generally try to avoid loneliness.
2. _____**A person**_____ who is lonely longs for a friend.
3. _____**People**_____ in my family are pretty outgoing.
4. My sister is in sales and loves to talk to _____**people**_____.
5. _____**A person**_____ I can always depend on is my brother.
6. I really appreciate _____**people**_____ who are open and honest.

Practice 5.2

Answers (Student's Book page 59)

1. The men who taught me yoga were Buddhist monks.
2. The teeth I broke are right in front.
3. The fish we ate last night were fresh from the sea.
4. The women I met last night looked much younger than their real ages.
5. The people who live next door to me are exercise fanatics.
6. The children who left their bikes here haven't come to get them.

SOME NONCOUNT NOUNS (Chart, Student's Book page 60)

Unlike the charts with singular and plural forms that begin Part 1 (Count Nouns, page 52) and Part 3 (Proper Nouns, page 63), this chart has only one column because noncount nouns do not have plural forms. The chart contains basic information that will be useful to students in Part 2 of this chapter.

Grammar Point 6	**Count vs. Noncount Nouns**

EXPLORING THE GRAMMAR POINT

Additional examples (Student's Book page 60)

- **Incorrect:** She brought *a luggage*.
  Correct: She brought *one piece of luggage*.
- **Incorrect:** I drank *three milks*.
  Correct: I drank *three glasses of milk*.

UNDERSTANDING THE GRAMMAR POINT

You might want to elicit additional examples for the chart.

Additional examples (Student's Book page 61)

Solids	pie, meat, thread
Liquids	tea, water, coffee
Gases	carbon monoxide, exhaust, breath
Particles	powder, pepper, dust
Materials	stainless steel, rubber, cotton
Fields of study	computer science, business, X-ray technology
Categories	hardware, fruit, china
Activities	running, skateboarding, chess
Feelings	guilt, sadness, hate, depression
Concepts	skill, intelligence, sleep

Practice 6.1

Answers (Student's Book page 61)

A Fishing Trip

Last spring, a friend and I spent a week fishing in the mountains. The ~~sceneries were~~ *scenery was*

amazing. The ~~snows~~ *snow* had recently melted and the ~~waters~~ *water* in the streams ~~were~~ *was* clear

and cold. The ~~weathers were~~ *weather was* perfect. Every day was full of ~~sunshines~~ *sunshine* and the ~~fishings~~ *fishing*

~~were~~ *was* great. The only problem was that my friend forgot to bring some of his fishing

~~equipments~~ *equipment*, so we had to take turns with mine. Oh, well. We remembered all our

~~clothings~~ *clothing*, we took plenty of ~~foods~~ *food*, and we had lots of ~~times~~ *time* to do everything we wanted.

Grammar Point 7 ▶ **Nouns That Can Be Count or Noncount**

EXPLORING THE GRAMMAR POINT

Additional examples (Student's Book page 62)

Count Nouns	**Noncount Nouns**
• Learning a new **skill** takes time.	Sailing requires a lot of **skill**.
• I bought a pumpkin **pie** for dessert.	Ellen hates pumpkin **pie**.
• There have been two great **loves** in his life.	**Love** makes the world go around.

UNDERSTANDING THE GRAMMAR POINT

Practice 7.1

Answers (Student's Book pages 62–63)

1. I love _____chocolate_____. I could eat it all day.

   I have to stop eating these _____chocolates_____.

   Go ahead, have _____a chocolate_____. One can't hurt.

2. I can see much better since I got _____glasses_____.

   Get _____a glass_____ and I'll give you some soda.

   Their new house is almost all made of _____glass_____.

3. I used to have _____a fear_____ of heights, but I got over it.

   For the first time, I felt real _____fear_____.

   He has so many _____fears_____ that he can hardly function.

4. My nephew got three _____footballs_____ for his birthday.

   I wish we had _____a football_____ so we could play.

   I don't really enjoy watching _____football_____ on TV.

5. There used to be successful _____businesses_____ all along this street.

   _____Business_____ is slow right now, but it will get better.

   I want to start _____a business_____ and work for myself.

6. I have to write _____a paper_____ for my English class.

   My father loves news. He reads two _____papers_____ every day.

   I don't have enough _____paper_____ to finish this letter.

SOME PROPER NOUNS (Chart, Student's Book page 63)

You might have students write sentences with the singular and plural forms in the chart. Have one or two students work at the board and correct their sentences with the whole class.

Additional examples (Student's Book page 63)

Singular	Plural
Mrs. Hopkins	the Hopkinses
December	Decembers
Thanksgiving	Thanksgivings

UNDERSTANDING THE GRAMMAR POINT

Notes on the charts (plural forms)

• *The Smiths* (to refer to a family) is very common; plural names of individuals (*the two Dannys*) are less common.

• Units of time and holidays are also common in both singular and plural forms (but decades, like *the 1930s,* are always plural).

• The other categories are seldom (or never) seen as plurals.

Practice 8.1

In this practice, all the proper nouns are singular.

Answers (Student's Book page 64)

A Run in the Park

~~The last sunday~~ [Last Sunday], the day before ~~memorial day~~ [Memorial Day], my friend ~~jake~~ [Jake] and I went for our usual run in ~~the pitt park~~ [Pitt Park]. The park is becoming very international because it attracts both immigrants and tourists. We heard people speaking languages from ~~the europe~~ [Europe] and the ~~latin america~~ [Latin America], but we also heard ~~the japanese~~ [Japanese], ~~the swahili~~ [Swahili], and some other languages we didn't recognize. This time we finished our run in a new way. We signed up for a class, ~~introduction to tai chi~~ [Introduction to Tai Chi], which was held right there in the park. There were students from probably ten different countries. It was a great way to end our workout. I don't know if ~~jake~~ [Jake] will keep going to the class, but I liked it a lot.

CHAPTER 4 REVIEW

Review Practice 4.1

Answers (Student's Book pages 65–66)

Getting Ready For the Beach

It's ~~june~~ [June] and my two best ~~friend~~ [friends] and I are thinking about the beach. We need to do

three ~~thing~~ [things] to get in shape for our ~~bikini~~ [bikinis]. First, we need to join a gym. We checked out

~~pumped~~ [Pumped] and we liked it. It has good ~~equipments~~ [equipment] and it doesn't cost too ~~many monies~~ [much money]. I

only need to buy a new pair of ~~shoe~~ [shoes] and [a] lock for my locker. Second, we need an eating

plan to help us lose ~~weights~~ [weight]. We chose ~~weight managers~~ [Weight Managers]. It's [a] good program and we all

think we can stick to it. You get to eat many different foods* including meat, fish, bread,

~~vegetable~~ [vegetables], and even a few ~~dessert~~ [desserts]. You have to drink eight ~~glass~~ [glasses] of ~~waters~~ [water] a day. That's

not easy, but I can do it. Third, we have to encourage each other. It's too hard to make

~~change~~ [changes] like these alone. But together, we can do it.

Food is not a noncount noun in this context.

Review Practice 4.2

Answers (Student's Book page 66)

My English Class

I am learning a lot in my English class this ~~semesters~~ [semester]. One ~~reasons~~ [reason] is that the

instructor gives us a lot of ~~homeworks~~ [homework]. We have to do two writing ~~assignment~~ [assignments] every

~~weeks~~ [week]. Also, we have learned a lot of new ~~vocabularies~~ [vocabulary]. We have to make ~~a lists~~ [lists (or a list)] of all

the new ~~word~~ [words] in every ~~books or articles~~ [book or article] we read. The third and most important ~~reasons~~ [reason]

why I am learning so much is that I am writing a term paper. Doing the ~~researches~~ [research]

for it has helped me learn how to use the library and the Internet to find ~~informations~~ [information].

Even though the ~~classes~~ [class] has given me a lot of extra ~~works~~ [work], I'm really glad I took my

counselor's ~~advices~~ [advice] and registered for it.

Nouns   **47**

Review Practice 4.3

Answers (Student's Book page 66)

The Six O'clock News Oral Essays

                              includes "oral essays"   topics

The six o'clock news often ~~include~~ ~~"oral essay"~~ on various ~~topic~~. Last night, for ~~an~~

example, the presentation discussed the importance of electronics. It seems that every

month   product

~~months~~ a new or improved electronic ~~products~~* comes out that many of us want to buy.

                         electronics

It's no wonder that ~~electronic~~ is a leading industry in our economy. The night before

           topic   education

last, the ~~topics~~ was economics, and last week they talked about ~~educations~~. Apparently,

               is   a   major   colleges

mathematics ~~are~~ becoming more popular ~~majors~~ for women in many ~~college~~. I appreciate

these   issues   lives

~~this~~ oral essays because they help me keep up on important ~~issue~~ in our daily ~~lifes~~.

                                       come

*Or ~~a~~ new or improved electronic products ~~comes~~ out

Articles

5

REFRESHING YOUR MEMORY

Answers (Student's Book page 67)

1. Which kind of noun almost always has to have a determiner? *A singular count noun*

2. Which kind of noun rarely takes an article? *A singular proper noun*

3. Which two kinds of noun don't usually take the article *a/an*? *A plural noun and a noncount noun*

EXPLORING THE TOPIC

Raymond Chandler, author of the excerpted passage "The Office in the Cahuenga Building," began writing crime novels in his late forties. His work defined the genre of hard-boiled detective fiction, and many feel he has never been surpassed. Chandler died in 1958. All seven of his novels are still in print.

Pronunciation note

In English, *Cahuenga* is pronounced /kə·wɛŋ′·gə/, with a silent *h* and stress on the second syllable.

The task previews some of the uses of *a / an* and *the* that will be discussed in the chapter.

Answers (Student's Book page 68)

Which version is correct? *Version 2*

Can you explain why the articles are correct in that version? Or do you just have a feeling that they are? *Students will probably be able to see that Version 2 is correct, but not be able to explain why. In fact, this is a "trick" question intended to focus their attention on the uses of articles; an adequate answer would be very long. The chapter will discuss each use of articles in Version 2.*

Grammar Point 1 ❯ **A vs. An**

This grammar point quickly covers the two forms of the indefinite article in case students need to be reminded of their use.

Practice 1.1

Answers (Student's Book page 69)

1. __a__ pistol   __an__ automatic pistol

2. __an__ office   __a__ dark office

3. __an__ expression   __a__ sad expression

4. __a__ marriage   __an__ unhappy marriage

5. __a__ divorce   __an__ uncontested divorce

6. __a__ room   __an__ empty room

A/An, *The*, and Common Focus

This grammar point introduces the terms *indefinite article* and *definite article,* and the idea of *common focus,* a central concept of this chapter.

EXPLORING THE GRAMMAR POINT
Additional examples
- He had **a table** and **a chair** in the waiting room. I moved **the chair** over to **the table** and sat down.
- **A woman** came in carrying **a large bag**. **The bag** was heavy. **The woman** could barely carry it.

UNDERSTANDING THE GRAMMAR POINT
The Student's Book states that *common focus* means that a writer and reader "share knowledge" of a noun. However, this knowledge is not what we usually mean by *knowledge*; it is confined to what is conveyed when the noun is used in communication, written or spoken. The concept should become clearer as students see how common focus is established in other ways in other grammar points in this chapter.

Practice 2.1
Answers (Student's Book page 70)

Find Her!

He opened ___a___ locked drawer and took out ___an___ envelope. He took
            (1)   (2)

___a___ photo and ___a___ telegram from ___the___ envelope and passed
   (3)   (4)   (5)

___the___ telegram across the desk. It had been sent from El Paso, Texas. I put
   (6)

___the___ telegram down on ___the___ desk.
   (7)   (8)

He pushed ___the___ photo across ___the___ desk. It was ___a___ snapshot
             (9)   (10)   (11)

showing ___a___ slim, small blonde and ___a___ tall, lean, dark, handsome man,
           (12)   (13)

about thirty-five. ___The___ blonde could have been anything from eighteen to forty. She
                       (14)

was that type. She wore ___a___ swimsuit, and ___the___ man wore trunks. They sat
                           (15)   (16)

against ___a___ striped beach umbrella on the sand. I put ___the___ snapshot down
           (17)   (18)

on top of ___the___ telegram.
              (19)

The with a Synonym, Part, or Closely Related Idea

EXPLORING THE GRAMMAR POINT

Additional examples (Student's Book page 70)

I bought **a new convertible** yesterday. Actually, **the car** is not new, but it is new to me. **The engine** is in good condition and **the odometer** only has 40,000 miles on it. **The owner** was an elderly woman who only drove it to the supermarket on Saturdays.

UNDERSTANDING THE GRAMMAR POINT

Note on *the keys*

Keys is, of course, a plural noun. The principle of common focus works in the same way for both singular and plural nouns in this context. *Key* (singular) would also take *the* here, and for the same reason.

Practice 3.1

Answers (Student's Book page 71)

1. She played __a__ Stradivarius violin. __An__ anonymous donor gave it to her. I don't know how much __the__ instrument was worth. Even __the__ bow was probably worth more than I made in a week.

2. I picked up __a__ magazine and tried to read, but I couldn't keep my eyes on __the__ page.

3. He showed me __a__ picture of Stella in __an__ ornate frame. At first, I didn't recognize her. Maybe __the__ photograph was a bad likeness, but I hadn't seen her for twenty years.

4. I made __an__ appointment to see Rogers at __a__ downtown hotel at 3:00. I was on time for __the__ meeting, but when I got to __the__ lobby, __the__ elevator was out of service. I started up __the__ stairs.

Practice 3.2

Answers (Student's Book page 71)

Number 200 was ^*a* tall, dark, old mansion with ^*a* garage in back. I tried ^*the* door. It was unlocked. I walked into ^*the* house, passed through ^*the* hall, and went downstairs to ^*the* basement. There was ^*an* iron bar on ^*the* floor near ^*a* large wooden crate. ~~Stain~~ *A stain* on ^*the* bar looked like blood. ~~Crate~~ *The crate* was open.

UNDERSTANDING THE GRAMMAR POINT

Additional examples (Student's Book page 72)

- I got into **the car that he pointed to**.
- She showed me **the gun in her purse**.

Practice 4.1

Answers (Student's Book page 72)

The j
1. ^Job of my dreams would let me work for six months and then take six months off.

The s
2. ^Smell of gunpowder was strong in the room.

the
3. The buzzer was on ^side of the desk where I could reach it easily.

the
4. I searched my pockets for ^phone number I had written down.

The c
5. ^Car he drove up in was new and expensive.

The m
6. ^Match I lit didn't help. I couldn't see anything.

The w
7. ^Window across from the door was open.

the
8. He never heard ^shot that killed him.

EXPLORING THE GRAMMAR POINT

Additional examples (Student's Book page 73)

- It was **the hottest day** of the summer.
- I turned off my phone. **The last thing** I needed was a phone call.

UNDERSTANDING THE GRAMMAR POINT

Practice 5.1

Answers (Student's Book page 74)

Going Up

The f
^First thing I had to do was find Skye's gun. This was Skye's building, but which was his

the
apartment? Knowing Skye, it would be ^most expensive one. That meant it had to be the

the   the   the
penthouse. I got on ^elevator and pushed ^button for ^top floor. Nothing happened. I pushed

it again. Then I noticed that the button had a keyhole next to it. The Floor was locked and I didn't have the/a key. This wasn't the worst thing that could have happened, but it was bad enough.

The with Natural Common Focus

EXPLORING THE GRAMMAR POINT

Additional examples (Student's Book page 74)
- **The sea** was empty all the way to **the horizon**.
- I drove to **the bank** and parked on **the street**.

UNDERSTANDING THE GRAMMAR POINT

Practice 6.1

Answers (Student's Book page 75)

Interlude

I went into ___the___ kitchen and drank ___a___ glass of cold water. Samuelson
                    1   2
would not call for hours and I was too restless to sit by ___the___ phone waiting for his
                                                            3
call. I got on ___the___ freeway and drove to ___the___ beach. ___The___ Ocean was
                4   5   6
calm and ___the___ sky was cloudless. It was too pretty an evening to go looking for
           7
trouble. I almost hoped Samuelson would have nothing to report. I parked on ___the___
                                                                               8
street and strolled along ___the___ boardwalk for a while. ___The___ Sun was setting
                            9   10
and ___the___ moon was already visible in ___the___ sky. I was hungry, but ___the___
      11   12   13
hot dog stand was closed. Further on, ___the___ visitor center was open. There was
                                        14
___a___ vending machine in ___the___ lobby. I went in and got ___a___ soda from
   15   16   17
___the___ machine.
   18

Note

Except for numbers 16 and 18, all *the* answers are examples of natural common focus. *The lobby* (16) is part of the visitor center (Grammar Point 3). *The machine* (18) is the second mention of this noun. Common focus was established at the first mention of *a vending machine* (Grammar Point 2).

No Article with Singular Nouns in Set Phrases

EXPLORING THE GRAMMAR POINT

Additional examples (Student's Book page 76)
- I was **at church** when you called Sunday morning.
- I don't like spinach much. **In fact**, I can't stand it.
- My first year of college, I lived **on campus**.

UNDERSTANDING THE GRAMMAR POINT

You might have students write sentences with the expressions in the chart. If done on the board, this could be a competition among teams.

Practice 7.1

Answers (Student's Book page 77)

No Sale

Last night at ~~the~~ dinner, my son was teasing me about being fat. Me, fat? I couldn't believe it, but I looked in the mirror, and he's right. In ~~the~~ high school I never had to think about my weight; in ~~the~~ fact, I was thin. Well, I'm forty now, so I guess I'm on ~~the~~ schedule for gaining weight. Anyway, this morning I looked in the newspaper and saw an ad for exercise bicycles on ~~the~~ sale. For a minute, I thought I might buy one, but I changed my mind. In the first place, my bedroom is too small for an exercise bike. But the main reason is that I'll never exercise at ~~the~~ home. I'm going to join a gym. Maybe I'll be in ~~a~~ better shape by the time we go to Florida on ~~a~~ vacation.

The **with Plural Nouns and Common Focus**

EXPLORING THE GRAMMAR POINT

Additional examples (Student's Book page 77)

In 1968, **astronauts** came within 70 miles of the surface of the Moon. **The astronauts** orbited the moon ten times before returning to Earth.

UNDERSTANDING THE GRAMMAR POINT

Plural nouns acquire common focus (and need *the*) in most of the same contexts as singular nouns. The chart describes contexts that were discussed for singular nouns in Grammar Points 2, 3, 4, and 5 of this chapter. (Plural nouns do not have natural common focus, as discussed for singular nouns in Grammar Point 6.)

Before teaching this grammar point, you might want to review *Chapter 4, Nouns*, Grammar Points 6 and 7 (pages 60–62), on noncount nouns.

EXPLORING THE GRAMMAR POINT

The first question can be answered based on information presented in *Chapter 4, Nouns*. The answers to the other questions can be inferred from guidelines already learned for singular nouns.

Answers (Student's Book page 78)

Which are count nouns and which are noncount?   *Numbers 3, 4, 5, and 6 are count nouns. Numbers 1, 2, and 7 are noncount.*

Numbers 1 and 7 do not have articles. Why?   *Number 1 is noncount, so it does not necessarily have an article. It is the first mention of* pizza *in the passage, so there is no common focus, and no article is needed. Number 7 has the determiner* Giovanni's, *so no article is needed.*

Number 2 has the article *the*. Why?   *Number 2 has common focus because it is followed by a phrase that limits its meaning and makes it specific: the pizza at Giovanni's. Noncount nouns need* the *when there is common focus and no other determiner.*

UNDERSTANDING THE GRAMMAR POINT

Noncount nouns acquire common focus (and need *the*) in many of the same contexts as singular nouns. The chart describes some of the contexts that were discussed for singular nouns in Grammar Points 2, 3, 4, and 5 of this chapter. Noncount nouns do not acquire common focus by being part of or closely related to a noun already mentioned (Grammar Point 3), and they do not have natural common focus (Grammar Point 6).

EXPLORING THE GRAMMAR POINT

Additional examples (Student's Book page 80)

- Our next-door neighbors are **the Lords**.
- **Dorothy Lord** has been my best friend since we moved here.
- We spent last Christmas in **the Bahamas**.
- This year we're staying home in **Pittsburgh**.

UNDERSTANDING THE GRAMMAR POINT

Practice 10.1

Answers (Student's Book page 80)

1. __The__ ~~T~~ea in the pot is fresh. I just made it.

2. __The__ ~~N~~ext music you hear will be __the__ Beatles.

3. Mr. Lee showed me an album of __—__ photographs. Some of __the__ photographs were of his wife.

4. _The_ Cars in the driveway were covered with mud and _the_ tires were flat.

5. _The_ Time that I spend here is always happy.

6. We went camping in _the_ Rockies.

7. We found two suitcases on the plane. _The_ bags were full of __—__ money.

8. _The_ Bartletts escaped with their lives. _The_ children were frightened, but unharmed.

9. __—__ Time flies.

10. This is _the_ most beautiful jewelry I have ever seen. _The_ earrings are especially fine.

Review Practice 5.1

Answers (Student's Book pages 81–82)

The Office in the Cahuenga Building (Continuation)

I had an office in the Cahuenga Building, sixth floor, two small rooms at the back. One I left open for a patient client to sit in, if I had a patient client. There was a buzzer on the door which I could switch on and off from my private office.

I looked into [the] reception room. It was empty of everything but [the] smell of dust. I unlocked [the] communicating door and went into [the] room beyond. Three hard chairs and [a] swivel chair, [a] desk with [a] glass top, five green filing cabinets, [a] calendar on [the] wall, [a] phone, [a] washbowl, and [a] carpet that was just something on the floor. Not beautiful, but better than [a] tent on [the] beach.

I hung my hat and coat on [the] hat rack, washed my face and hands in cold water, and lifted [the] phone book onto [the] desk. I wrote down Elisha Morningstar's address and [the] phone number that went with it. I had my hand on [the] instrument when I remembered that I hadn't switched on [the] buzzer in [the] other room. I reached over [the] side of [the] desk and clicked it on. Someone had just opened [the] door of [the] outer office.

Review Practice 5.2

Answers (Student's Book page 82)

Placement

The [P]lacement office is on [the] main floor, near [the] front of [the] building. I glance at [the] bulletin board in [the] hallway, but I keep walking. There is not [a] single notice on [the] board. There is no job market at this time of the year.

Madeline Skinner has run Placement here for decades. She's very good at what she does. If [a] Memphis State graduate is in charge of recruiting for [a] big firm, and [the] big firm has too few Memphis grads, then Madeline calls [the] president of [the] university and [the] president visits [the] big firm and takes care of [the] problem.

             the   **the**   **a**

She's standing by ⌄ water cooler watching ⌄ door, as if she's waiting for me. She has ⌄ cup

                                       the

of water in one hand and she points with ⌄ cup to her office. "Let's talk in here."

Review Practice 5.3

Answers (Student's Book page 83)

A Lie and a Half

A man returned to his hometown after a long trip. He told his neighbor, "On my trip

                                The

I saw a huge ship with gigantic sails. ~~A~~ ship was bigger than anything anyone could

                                      the   **the**

imagine. A young man walked from one end of ~~a~~ ship to ⌄ other end. His hair and beard

turned white before he got there!"

The m

   ~~M~~an's neighbor replied, "That's not so remarkable. I once passed through ⌄ tremendous

                                        a

The   **the**   **the**   **a**   **the**

forest. ~~A~~ forest had ⌄ tallest trees in ~~a~~ world. In fact, ⌄ bird tried to fly to ⌄ top. It flew for ten

                          the

years and only made it to ⌄ halfway point."

                a   **the**

   "You're ~~the~~ terrible liar," said ⌄ first man. "That simply can't be possible."

                                          the   (OR **the tree**)

   "Why not?" asked his neighbor. "Where do you think ~~a~~ ship you saw got a tree for

its mast?"

Review Practice 5.4

Answers (Student's Book page 83)

                    the   **the**

1. I had to stop at ⌄ store to get bread on my way home. I had ~~a~~ time, so I went to ⌄ Polish

                                    the   **the**

   bakery on ~~the~~ Tenth Street. In my opinion, ⌄ bread there is ~~a~~ best bread in town*.

The w

2. ~~W~~eather was terrible. First there was fog, and later there was freezing rain.

The   **the**

3. ⌄ Oranges are four towns near Newark, New Jersey. I have lived in ⌄ Oranges all my

                                      The

   life—first in Orange and later in East Orange. ⌄ Orange I live in now is West Orange.

                                                the

4. I took too much luggage when I went to Africa, and ⌄ suitcases were too full. I had

                        a   **a**

enough equipment for ⌄ six-month expedition, and I was only going for ⌄ month.

5. My best friend in elementary school* was Adam McCartney. My name is Adam too, so
   everyone called us ^the^ Adams. We spent all our free time together, and ^the^ McCartneys were

   like my second family.

6. Love is war.

7. I have to take Advanced Algebra 1 next year. Luckily, I don't have to take Advanced

   Algebra 2. I hate math.

8. Give me ^a^ big enough lever and ~~the~~ ^a^ place to stand, and I can move ^the^ earth.

In town is a set phrase that does not use *the*. *In elementary school* is a set phrase too, like
in school.

SECTION 2 REVIEW

REFRESHING YOUR MEMORY

Answers (Student's Book page 84)

1. The plural of *party* is *parties*. Why? *Party is singular and it ends in* -ty *(a consonant + y). Form the plural by changing the* y *to* i *and adding* -es.

2. Which plural is irregular: *boxes, wives, women*? *Women is irregular. It does not end in* -s.

   What are the guidelines for the two that are regular? *Box ends in* -x. *Form the plural by adding* -es. *Wife ends in* -ife. *Form the plural by changing* -ife *to* -ives.

3. In which sentence is *food* a noncount noun?
   a. I never say no to food.
   b. I have tried every food I have ever been served.
   c. Some foods are just not good for you.

   Food is noncount in sentence (a).

4. In each of the three sentences above, why doesn't *food* need an article?
   a. *Noncount nouns do not take an article unless there is common focus. There is no common focus here.*
   b. *Food is singular. It needs a determiner, but not necessarily an article. Every is a determiner.*
   c. *Plural nouns do not take an article unless there is common focus. There is no common focus here.*

5. What is common focus? *Common focus is shared knowledge. A noun has common focus when it has specific or definite meaning for both the writer (or speaker) and the reader.*

   What article is used for a noun that has common focus? *The definite article* the

6. Which phrase is wrong: *on the sale, the last sale, the best sale*? Why? *On the sale is wrong. On sale is a set phrase comprising a preposition + a noun. In such set phrases, the noun does not take an article.*

Section Review Practice 2.1

Suggested procedure

• On the board or as a handout, supply the paragraph with blanks instead of articles, as below. Have students fill in the missing articles and go over the answers.

The Defective Stereo

I bought _____ new personal stereo and _____ package of CDs last week. When I got home, _____ stereo didn't work. _____ power switch was defective. I couldn't find _____ receipt, so _____ salesperson wouldn't exchange it for me. Later, I found _____ receipt under _____ box of CDs.

• Have students do the matching exercise either in pairs (if they have handouts) or all together (if the passage is on the board).

• Let them discuss their answers. It is more important that they know which article to use than that they be absolutely sure of the reason for each one.

Answers (Student's Book page 84)

Why is *the* used with the nouns in italics? Write the letter of the correct answer.

1. __a__ the stereo
2. __c__ the power switch
3. __d__ the receipt
4. __e__ the salesperson
5. __b__ the box

Section Review Practice 2.2

Answers (Student's Book page 85)

My Sister's Sweet Tooth

My sister's refrigerator is full of ~~the~~ junk food. ~~T~~op shelf is loaded with can^s of soda. On

^the next shelf, three box^es from three bakery^ies are stacked together. They contain a pie and two

cake^s. Next to^the boxes is^a carton of milk—chocolate milk. In^the vegetable bin, several container^s

of pudding crowd out a few old carrot^s in^the back of the drawer. Several jar^s of ~~the~~ jam and

~~the~~ jelly sit next to^a jar of butterscotch topping. At least in^the freezer, there is some real

food~~s~~: two TV dinner^s. Next to^the dinner^s are four pint^s of ice cream. I'm having dinner at my

sister's on Friday. I wonder what^the menu is going to be.

Section Review Practice 2.3

Answers (Student's Book page 85)

This Is Not My Grandmother

I'm not very attentive. That's why I sometimes find myself in awkward situation^s. One

day when I was^a child, my grandmother and I decided to visit her sister. We didn't have

^a car so we took^the subway. I was supposed to hold^my grandmother's hand. We were standing

on^the platform and waiting for^the train. She gave me^a piece of cand~~ies~~y and I released^her hand to

unwrap it. Just then^the train came in and I grabbed^her hand in order not to get lost. There

were^a lot of people~~s~~ in^the car.

After a few minutes, I asked her, "When will we get there?" A ~~M~~man's deep voice

answered, "I don't know." Because I was small, my eyes were at^the level of^the person's stomach. In astonishment, I looked up, but all I could see was ^(a) huge stomach. I couldn't

see the face. Then I looked at ^(the) hand. It was not ^(my) grandmother's hand! Instead I was

holding ^(the) hand of ^(a) stranger. In a panic, I looked around for ^(my) grandmother. She was standing

right behind me and smiling. I still remember how I felt ^(that) day. After that, I was always

careful to stay with ^(the) person who accompanied me.

Section Review Practice 2.4

Answers (Student's Book page 86)

A Dizzy Day

I still remember ~~a~~ ^(the) worst day of frustration in my life~~s~~. I was frustrated by my own

failure. Almost two year ^(s) ago, one day I felt dizzy because of influenza, but I went to ~~the~~

school anyway. I had ~~the~~ computer class, and I was making ^(a) home page with ^(a) classmate. I

felt short of breath, but it was raining, so I couldn't open ^(the / a) window in ^(the) computer lab.

^(My) ~~C~~classmate said, "You look pale! Are you OK? You should go home."

I appreciated her concern, but we had to submit ^(the) assignment by ~~a~~ ^(the) next week, so I

couldn't go home. In those days, I worked at ^(a) restaurant part time. When we finished

in ^(the) computer lab, ^(the) time was 4:00 P.M. It was time to start work at ^(the) restaurant. I went to

^(the) restaurant in a hurry, and I still felt dizzy because I had run a lot. Anyway, while I was

working, I spilled ~~a~~ tea on a customer and ^(her) dress got wet.

I said, "Sorry," but in fact, I didn't understand what had happened. I just felt dizzy.

The manager came and apologized to her. I just watched ^(the) conversation. Then he said to

me, "You should go home today." So I went home. ~~V~~ ^(The) ^(v) Very next day, I recovered, so I went

to ^(the) restaurant and apologized to ^(the) boss. "I am so sorry. I made ^(a) big mistake."

"It's OK. Everyone makes mistakes. Don't worry about it."

Since ^(that) experience, I have taken care of ^(my) health. If I get sick, I may cause ~~the~~ trouble

for other people. I think ~~the~~ good health is ~~a~~ ^(the) most important thing of all. And I want to

forget ^(that) experience as soon as possible.

The Simple Present and the Present Progressive

6

EXPLORING THE TOPIC

The excerpt "Mr. Green" is from Robert Olen Butler's collection of stories *A Good Scent from a Strange Mountain*. The stories are about Vietnamese expatriates living in Louisiana. The book won the Pulitzer Prize. Butler speaks fluent Vietnamese, spent a year in Vietnam during the war there, and lives in Lake Charles, Louisiana. The World Parrot Trust works to ensure the survival of parrot species in the wild, and aids the welfare of captive parrots everywhere. "Parrot Project in Mexico" is a brief announcement of one of their projects.

The questions focus students' attention on aspects of the meaning and form of the simple present and the present progressive tenses.

Answers (Student's Book page 88)

1. Which passage is about current events? *"Parrot Project in Mexico"*
   Which is about events that happen repeatedly over time? *"Mr. Green"*

2. How are the italicized verbs in "Parrot Project in Mexico" different from the italicized verbs in "Mr. Green?" *In "Parrot Project," the verbs have at least two words: the first word is a form of* be, *and the last word ends with* -ing. *In "Mr. Green," the verbs are just one word and they do not end with* -ing.

Grammar Point 1 ⟩ **The Form of the Simple Present**

UNDERSTANDING THE GRAMMAR POINT

Additional examples (for the chart)

Other verbs that work well for examples (including with *it* and for sentences like those in Practice 1.1) are *sleep* and *wait*.

Practice 1.1

Answers (Student's Book page 89)

1. You __talk__ too much.
2. Bradley __talks__ to himself all the time.
3. Some domesticated parrots __talk__ .
4. You've got to hear this bird. It __talks__ !
5. My little sister __talks__ constantly.
6. My mother and I __talk__ every day.

7. I __talk__ on the phone at least three hours a day.

8. My parents never __talk__ about money in front of me.

9. My family* always __talks__ a lot at dinner.

10. Rachel __talks__ too fast. I can't understand her.

*In American English, collective nouns like *family, team,* and *company* take singular verb forms. (However, subsequently, they are usually referred to with plural pronouns, which take plural verb forms: His **family is** from Texas originally. **They have** relatives in Dallas.)

Grammar Point 2 — Forming the Third Person Singular

"Third person singular" is shorthand for "third person singular in the simple present tense."

UNDERSTANDING THE GRAMMAR POINT

The guidelines are for verbs that are regular in the simple present tense. Irregular verbs are discussed in Grammar Point 3.

Grammar Point 3 — Irregular Verbs

UNDERSTANDING THE GRAMMAR POINT

Generally we think of verbs as being irregular in their past tense forms and / or past participles. Most of the verbs in *Appendix B, Common Irregular Verbs* (pages 274–276), are regular in their present tense forms. *Say /says* is irregular in the pronunciation of its third person singular form, like *do / does.*

Practice 3.1

This brings together material from Grammar Points 1, 2, and 3. The verbs in answers 5, 7, and 13 are irregular.

Answers (Student's Book pages 91–92)

Jason and His Parents

Six-year-old Jason (idolize) _____idolizes_____ his parents, David and

1

Hideko. David (own) _____owns_____ a computer software business. Hideko

2

(study) _____studies_____ business management at Florida State University.

3

When Hideko (finish) _____finishes_____ her classes each day, she (go)

4

_____goes_____ home. After she (greet) _____greets_____ Jason and

5   6

(have) _____has_____ a snack with him, she (study) _____studies_____ for

7   8

an hour while Jason plays with his toys. After David (arrive) _____arrives_____ and

9

(greet) _____ **greets** _____ his family, he (spend) _____ **spends** _____ a short
                    10   11

time at his computer. Later, David (fix) _____ **fixes** _____ dinner with Hideko. After
                                                      12

dinner, one parent usually (do) _____ **does** _____ the dishes while the other (help)
                                              13

_____ **helps** _____ Jason get ready for bed. Jason (wash) _____ **washes** _____
            14   15

his face, (brush) _____ **brushes** _____ his teeth, and (get) _____ **gets** _____
                            16   17

into his pajamas. Later, David usually (tell) _____ **tells** _____ Jason a
                                                          18

story or (play) _____ **plays** _____ a game with him. Sometimes Jason
                          19

(watch) _____ **watches** _____ the news on television with his mother and (fall)
                      20

_____ **falls** _____ asleep in her arms. David (carry) _____ **carries** _____ Jason
            21   22

to bed and (kiss) _____ **kisses** _____ him goodnight.
                            23

Writing Assignment 1

Suggested procedure

- Ask students to find the five verbs in the third person singular, simple present tense (is, does, dusts, vacuums, and changes).
- Make sure students understand what is going on in the comic strip. Elicit a synopsis: Lois, the mother, works from home. Hi, the father, helps around the house. He does the laundry, dusts, vacuums, and changes the baby's diapers. He also fixes dinner, but he isn't a good cook and he burns it.
- Prepare students for the writing task by relating it to the story in the comic strip.

Grammar Point 4 **Habits and Customs**

UNDERSTANDING THE GRAMMAR POINT

In "Mr. Green," the italicized words describe actions that the parrot and the woman do again and again over time.

Additional examples (Student's Book page 92)

Use the comic strip in Writing Assignment 1 on page 92 in the Student's Book. Ask students which verbs describe actions that the father, Hi, does again and again over time (does laundry, dusts, vacuums, changes diapers).

Grammar Point 5 **Time Markers for Habits and Customs**

EXPLORING THE GRAMMAR POINT

This grammar point can be taught inductively with books open to "Mr. Green" (page 88), not turning to page 93 until you refer to the chart in Understanding the Grammar Point.

UNDERSTANDING THE GRAMMAR POINT

The explanation assumes that students know the meanings of the time markers in the chart. You may want to review their meanings for your students before teaching the grammar point.

Additional examples (Student's Book page 93)

Frequency adverbs go after the verb *be*.

- I **am frequently** late for appointments.
- People **are often** annoyed with me for that.

With other verbs, they go between the subject and the verb.

- **I sometimes get** to class late.
- **I always apologize** when I arrive late.

Some frequency adverbs can also go before the subject.

- **Frequently / Often / Usually / Sometimes Rachel and I** have coffee after class.

Practice 5.1

You could have students think of sentences about themselves, then interview each other to get sentences about another person. Some of the sentences could be written on the board and corrected there. Students' answers will vary.

Suggested answers (Student's Book page 94)

1. I don't usually drink coffee at night.
   My friend Nelson drinks three or four cups of coffee every morning.
2. I never take the bus to work. I always drive.
   Dave often takes the bus to work when his car won't start.
3. I never wear black. It looks terrible on me.
   Elaine wears black almost every day. She thinks it looks cool.
4. I always watch the Superbowl on TV.
   My wife never watches sports on TV, not even the Superbowl.
5. I usually buy one newspaper in the morning and read other papers online at night.
   My dad buys a newspaper every morning, but he doesn't often finish it.

Grammar Point 6	**General Truths**

EXPLORING THE GRAMMAR POINT

Additional examples (Student's Book page 94)

- Water **boils** at 100° Centigrade.
- The house **has** three bedrooms.
- I **love** the city, but my husband **loves** the country.
- Everything **happens** for a reason.
- I **go** to the gym four times a week. (habitual action)

Practice 6.1

Answers (Student's Book page 95)

Better Diets for Parrots

A wild parrot (live) _____**lives**_____ in the rain forest. It (spend)

_____**spends**_____ its life in the trees where it (eat) _____**eats**_____ and

is safe from predators. Fresh green foods (make up) _____**make up**_____ most

of the wild parrot's diet. The rain forest (contain) _____**contains**_____ a huge

variety of edible green plants. Parrots (consume) _____**consume**_____ all parts of

these plants, as well as nuts, seeds, fruits and berries. Some of these foods (supply)

_____**supply**_____ small amounts of protein and fat.

The diet of captive parrots (be) _____**is***_____ very different. Most

birdkeepers (feed) _____**feed**_____ a "parrot mixture" of mostly seeds, nuts,

and grains. Unfortunately, this (produce) _____**produces**_____ a high-fat, high-

protein diet completely unlike the parrot's natural diet. It (lack) _____**lacks**_____

essential vitamins, minerals, and fiber. This (be) _____**is**_____ why we (see)

_____**see**_____ so many overweight and malnourished parrots in captivity.

*You may need to explain that in number 8, the verb is singular because the subject is *diet*, not *parrots*.

Grammar Point 7	**The Form of the Present Progressive**

UNDERSTANDING THE GRAMMAR POINT

Suggestion for using the charts

- With books closed, write the guidelines for each chart on the board. Include one example of each (base form and -*ing* form).
- Write the base forms of one or two other verbs from each chart on the board in an alphabetical list.
- Have students (individually or in pairs) write down the -*ing* forms of each verb and then open their books to check their work. Alternatively, call on students to write the -*ing* forms next to the base forms on the board.

Contractions vs. Full Forms

Although full forms are preferred in academic writing, you may want your students to know the conventions for using contractions.

UNDERSTANDING THE GRAMMAR POINT

The chart shows contractions of *be* with pronoun subjects, the most common use of them in writing. *Nitty Gritty Grammar* does not discuss the use of contractions with common or proper noun subjects. Contractions with such subjects tend to make the writing seem still less formal—more like speech.

Practice 8.1

Students are expected to write contractions with pronoun subjects, but use full forms with other subjects.

Answers (Student's Book page 97)

1. The sun (shine) _____is shining_____ brightly, and it (get) _____'s getting_____ hot.
2. It's afternoon now and the lions (not move) _____aren't moving_____.
3. They (sleep) _____'ve sleeping_____ in the back of their enclosure.
4. One young lion (rest) _____is resting_____ on her back with her feet in the air.
5. A family on vacation (take) _____is taking_____ a tour with a guide from the zoo.
6. The guide (explain) _____is explaining_____ about the lions' social behavior.
7. The adults (listen) _____are listening_____, but the children (not pay) _____are not paying_____ attention.
8. They (try) _____'ve trying_____ to see the monkeys in the next enclosure.

Grammar Point 9 | **Using the Present Progressive to Express the Moment of Communication**

UNDERSTANDING THE GRAMMAR POINT

Practice 8.1, page 97, provides examples of this use of the present progressive.

Practice 9.1

Students are required to observe the real world around them and describe the actions they see with the present progressive. You might begin by having students brainstorm a list of possible verbs (base forms) on the board. Remind them that some of their sentences can be negative. Students' answers will vary.

Suggested verbs

look around, watch, write, read, think, talk, eat, chew gum, sit still, walk around, look out the window, erase a mistake, borrow a pen / piece of paper / pencil / eraser, wait for us to finish

EXPLORING THE GRAMMAR POINT

Additional examples (Student's Book page 98)

- **Incorrect:** She**'s loving** her new cookbook. It**'s containing** easy recipes and **having** lots of helpful photographs.

   Correct: She **loves** her new cookbook. It **contains** easy recipes and **has** lots of helpful photographs.

UNDERSTANDING THE GRAMMAR POINT

Additional examples (Student's Book page 99) of verbs that can be either active or stative

- **Stative:** My brother **has** blue eyes. (ownership / possession)

  Stative: I **don't have** twenty dollars. (ownership / possession)

- **Active:** Lizzy is excited. Her cat **is having** kittens. (action)

  Active: Sorry about the noise! My neighbors **are having** a party. (action)

Practice 10.1

Answers (Student's Book page 99)

1. I (like) _____ like _____ cats a lot.
2. I (think) _____ think _____ cats make the best pets.
3. I (have) _____ have _____ a big, handsome, black cat.
4. Actually, I (think) _____ 'm thinking _____ about getting another cat.
5. My cat (not look) _____ isn't looking _____ out the window right now.
6. He (sleep) _____ 's sleeping _____ on the desk next to me.
7. He (look) _____ looks _____ very relaxed.
8. He (be) _____ 's _____ a great cat.
9. He (understand) _____ understands _____ me.
10. Maybe I (not need) _____ don't need _____ another cat.

UNDERSTANDING THE GRAMMAR POINT

The italicized verbs in "Parrot Project in Mexico" (page 88) exemplify the use of the present progressive to describe temporary situations. Teaching Grammar Point 11 and Grammar Point 12 together may give students a better feel for this meaning of the tense.

Additional examples (Student's Book page 100)

Andrew **is living** in Chile. He **is working** in the Santiago office, **learning** Spanish and **traveling** around the country. Next year he will take over as sales manager for Argentina, Chile, and Peru.

Time Markers for Temporary Situations

UNDERSTANDING THE GRAMMAR POINT

The time markers in the chart can go at the beginning of a sentence or at the end.

• At the moment, I'm living in Reno. / I'm living in Reno at the moment.

• This week, I'm not driving to work. / I'm not driving to work this week.

At this point, you might want to contrast the use of the present progressive for temporary situations with the use of the simple present for habits and customs. Use the suggested examples below, or use true sentences about yourself and your students.

Suggested examples (Student's Book page 100) for contrasting the present progressive and the simple present

• Jody **is** a dancer. Currently, she **is also working** as a pre-school teacher.

• Ed usually **shares** an apartment with a roommate, but right now he**'s living** with his parents.

• I **study** hotel management at City College. I**'m taking** five courses this semester.

• Business Edge, Inc., **conducts** surveys for businesses. This month they**'re doing** a survey for the public library.

Practice 12.1

Students are required to think about their own lives and report several things they are doing currently that they do not usually do. If you contrasted the simple present with the present progressive as suggested in Grammar Point 12, students are already prepared to do this. If not, you might wish to introduce this task in a similar fashion.

Remind students that some of their sentences can be negative, and that they must not use stative verbs (listed on page 99 of the Student's Book). You could have them think of sentences, then interview each other, write down their partner's answers, and report some of them to the class. Some sentences could also be written on the board and corrected there. Students' answers will vary.

Practice 12.2

Answers (Student's Book page 101)

1. Sandra (take) _____is taking Art History 201_____ this term.

   She (also take) _____is also taking Cell Biology_____.

2. Mark (live) _____is living in Oaxaca, Mexico,_____ now.

3. Ruth Ann (spend a lot of time) _____is spending a lot of time with Alan_____ these days.

   She (not go out) _____isn't going out with Jake_____ very often.

4. Rita (work) _____isn't working_____ right now.

   She (look for a job) _____'s looking for a job_____.

Review Practice 6.1

Answers (Student's Book page 103)

Laura

Laura has a heavy schedule this semester. She ~~takes~~ *is taking* a chemistry class, two English

classes, an art class, and a business class. Also, she ~~watches~~ *is watching* her neighbor's house

for a month while her neighbor is away, and she ~~babysits~~ *is babysitting* for her sister's children. At

this moment it is 8:00 on a Thursday evening, and Laura ~~studies~~ *is studying* for a chemistry test

tomorrow. Right now she ~~tries~~ *is trying* to study and keep an eye on the kids at the same time.

The kids ~~watch~~ *are watching* cartoons. However, Laura ~~doesn't concentrate~~ *isn't concentrating* on her chemistry notes.

Instead, she ~~watches~~ *is watching* the cartoons.

Review Practice 6.2

Answers (Student's Book page 103)

Louise

This week, Louise is doing something entirely different from what she ~~is usually doing~~ *usually does*

in her daily routine. In her normal routine, she ~~is getting up~~ *gets up* at 6:00 A.M. on weekdays.

She ~~is almost always having~~ *almost always has* breakfast at 7:00 and ~~reading~~ *reads* the newspaper while she ~~is~~

~~eating~~ *eats*. She ~~is needing~~ *needs* to leave the house before 7:45. She ~~is usually going~~ *usually goes* to work with

a co-worker and ~~spending~~ *spends* the entire day at the office.

This week, however, Louise's schedule ~~is being~~ *is* entirely different. To start with, she is

getting up and having breakfast at 10:00 or later, and she is not reading the newspaper.

Instead, she is reading a detective novel. Also, she is spending all her time with her

husband and children. They ~~are having~~ *have* time to relax and enjoy each other's company.

They ~~are swimming~~ *swim* in the ocean every day and ~~going~~ *go* out to dinner every night. You have

probably guessed that Louise ~~is being~~ *is* on vacation this week.

Review Practice 6.3

Answers (Student's Book page 104)

Second-Hand Smoke

    Second-hand cigarette smoke harms nonsmokers. Much of this smoke ~~is rising~~ *rises* off the end of a burning cigarette. Scientists ~~are calling~~ *call* it *sidestream smoke.* This type of smoke ~~contain~~ *contains* twice as much tar and nicotine as smokers inhale. Smokers ~~are puffing~~ *puff* through a filter, but sidestream smoke ~~is not go~~ *does not go* through a filter. Studies ~~warns~~ *warn* against the dangers of second-hand smoke. It ~~is killing~~ *kills* about 53,000 nonsmokers in the U.S. each year. It ~~cause~~ *causes* about 37,000 deaths a year from heart disease. It ~~is also bringing about~~ *also brings about*

20 percent of all lung cancer in nonsmokers. As a result of these studies, many people ~~wants~~ *want* stricter laws against smoking in public places.

The Simple Past and the Past Progressive

7

EXPLORING THE TOPIC

The author of the excerpt "Memorial for Deng Xiaoping," Adam Hessler, was a Peace Corps Volunteer in Fuling from 1996 to 1998. Fuling is located on the Yangtze River, and much of the city that Hessler describes was inundated after the Three Gorges Dam was completed. This enormous flood-control and power-generating project flooded much of the Yangtze Valley.

The questions draw students' attention to the simple past and the past progressive, showing examples of the two tenses in an authentic context.

Answers (Student's Book pages 105–106)

Which are simple past verbs, and which are past progressive verbs? *The past progressive verbs are* was wiping, (was) sobbing, *and* were crying. *The other italicized verbs are in the simple past.*

What is different about the verbs in the past progressive? *They end in* -ing.

From *Chapter 6, The Simple Present and the Present Progressive,* students know that the present progressive tense has *-ing* endings. They should be able to infer that the verbs in the passage with *-ing* endings are examples of the past progressive tense.

Grammar Point 1 | The Form of the Simple Past

This grammar point provides guidelines for writing regular past tense forms. It does not address the pronunciation of past tense endings. However, if you wish to teach it, there are examples of all three pronunciations (/əd/, /d/, and /t/) in the past tense forms in the chart.

UNDERSTANDING THE GRAMMAR POINT

Suggestion for using the charts

- With books closed, write the guideline for each chart on the board. Include one example of each (base form and past tense).
- Write the base forms of one or two other verbs from each chart on the board in an alphabetical list.
- Have students (individually or in pairs) write down the past tense forms of each verb and then open their books to check their work. Alternatively, call on students to write the past tense forms next to the base forms on the board.

Practice 1.1

Advise students to refer to the charts in Grammar Point 1 as they work.

Answers (Student's Book page 108)

Marilu's Quinceañera

Marilu (celebrate) _____celebrated_____ her *quinceañera* last week. The night before
1

her birthday, a *mariachi* band (assemble) _____assembled_____ under her window
2

and (serenade) _____serenaded_____ her. Marilu (open) _____opened_____ her
3   4

window and (look out) _____looked out_____ while they sang. On Saturday evening,
5

the festivities (start) _____started_____ with a special mass at Marilu's church. She
6

(invite) _____invited_____ only her family, godparents, and closest friends to the
7

church. She wore a long pink dress and (carry) _____carried_____ flowers.
8

Marilu's parents (rent) _____rented_____ a hall for a party after the mass,
9

and almost a hundred people (attend) _____attended_____. The party (start)
10

_____started_____ when Marilu and her friends (arrive) _____arrived_____
11   12

from the church. First everyone (enjoy) _____enjoyed_____ a wonderful meal and
13

Marilu (receive) _____received_____ some traditional gifts. After that, Marilu (dance)
14

_____danced_____ the first dance with her father, and then everyone (party)
15

_____partied_____ all night.
16

Grammar Point 2 ▶ Irregular Past Tense Verbs

UNDERSTANDING THE GRAMMAR POINT

Be is the only verb that has two forms in the simple past. You might want to introduce the
verbs in the chart with books closed. Write the base forms on the board and have students
supply as many of the past tense forms as they can.

Practice 2.1

Two irregular verbs (*was* and *stood*) are each used twice in "Memorial for Deng Xiaoping."
You may wish to refer students to *Appendix B, Common Irregular Verbs* (Student's Book
pages 274–276). *Broadcast* and *lead* are not in that list, however. You might have students
share their dictionaries to find those base forms.

Answers (Student's Book page 109)

Base form	Past tense	Base form	Past tense
be	was	stand	stood
broadcast	broadcast	sit down	sat down
meet	met	speak	spoke
lead	led	keep	kept
give	gave	be	was

Practice 2.2

All but four of the verbs are listed in *Appendix B, Common Irregular Verbs* (pages 274–276). The four are numbers 6 (*set / set*), 11 (*hit / hit*), 21 (*speed / sped*), and 24 (*sink / sank*).

Answers (Student's Book pages 110–111)

(The underlined time markers are the answers for Practice 5.1 on Student's Book page 114.)

Amelia Earhart

In 1928, Amelia Earhart (win) _____ won _____ international recognition
1

as the first woman to cross the Atlantic Ocean by air. After that, people all over

the world frequently (read) _____ read _____ about her in the newspaper.
2

In 1932, Earhart (fly) _____ flew _____ solo across the Atlantic. She (be)
3

_____ was _____ the first woman and second person to do so (the first person
4

was Charles Lindbergh). In 1935, she (become) _____ became _____ the first person
5

to fly solo across the Pacific, from Honolulu, Hawaii, to Oakland, California. She also

(set) _____ set _____ the women's record for the fastest nonstop transcontinental
6

flight (from Los Angeles, California, to Newark, New Jersey). Later, she (break)

_____ broke _____ her own record.
7

In March, 1935, Amelia Earhart (begin) _____ began _____ her first attempt at an
8

around-the-world flight. However, soon after the plane (take off) _____ took off _____,
9

it (go) _____ went _____ out of control and (hit) _____ hit _____ the
10   11

ground. No one was hurt. In June, 1937, Earhart (leave) _____ left _____ on her
12

second attempt to fly around the world. On July 2, 1937, when the trip was almost over,

she (get) _____ got _____ into trouble. Airport personnel in New Guinea (think)
13

_____thought_____ that she (have) _____had_____ enough fuel when she
      14   15

took off from there. However, in one of her last radio communications, Earhart (say)

_____said_____ that her gas (be) _____was_____ low. Soon after
      16   17

that, the airport (lose) _____lost_____ radio contact with her. No one (know)
                                   18

_____knew_____ where she was or what had happened to her.
      19

Bad weather (make) _____made_____ visibility very poor that day. One theory
                         20

is that the plane (speed) _____sped_____ right past its destination at Howland
                         21

Island, northwest of Hawaii. If the plane (run out) _____ran out_____ of gas, it
                                         22

probably (fall) _____fell_____ into the sea and (sink) _____sank_____.
            23   24

In any case, no one ever (find) _____found_____ Earhart's plane, and no one
                         25

knows for sure what happened to Amelia Earhart.

Grammar Point 3 ▸ Negatives in the Simple Past

EXPLORING THE GRAMMAR POINT

Additional examples (Student's Book page 111)

- My birthday party **was not** on my birthday.
- Some of my friends **were not able** to come that day.
- I **did not want** to leave anyone out.

UNDERSTANDING THE GRAMMAR POINT

Additional examples

- My birthday party **wasn't** on my birthday.
- Some of my friends **weren't able** to come that day.
- I **didn't want** to leave anyone out.

Practice 3.1

Answers (Student's Book page 112)

1. Amelia Earhart was not the first woman to fly solo across the Atlantic.
2. People did not hear about Amelia Earhart before 1928.
3. Charles Lindbergh did not fly solo across the Pacific in 1935.
4. Earhart's planes were not always safe.

5. Earhart's two attempts to fly around the world weren't successful.

6. The second attempt wasn't an easy trip.

7. Her last radio communications didn't give her location.

8. She didn't reach her destination.

Grammar Point 4 ▶ Actions Completed in the Past

UNDERSTANDING THE GRAMMAR POINT

Although the examples do not contain time markers (which are introduced in Grammar Point 5), the time is clear and specific—the time of Marilu's *quinceañera* (page 108).

Grammar Point 5 ▶ Time Markers for the Simple Past

EXPLORING THE GRAMMAR POINT

Additional questions (Student's Book page 113) about "Amelia Earhart" (based on paragraph 2)

- When did Amelia Earhart begin her first attempt to fly around the world?
- When did her plane go out of control?

UNDERSTANDING THE GRAMMAR POINT

Answers to the additional questions

- **In March, 1935,** Amelia Earhart began her first attempt at an around-the-world flight.
- However, **soon after** the plane took off, it went out of control and hit the ground.

Practice 5.1

Answers (Student's Book page 114)

See the answer key for Practice 2.2 (pages 75–76 in this Teacher's Manual). The time markers for Practice 5.1 are underlined.

Grammar Point 6 ▶ The Form of the Past Progressive

EXPLORING THE GRAMMAR POINT

Additional examples (Student's Book page 114)

There was a parade for the city's winning soccer team yesterday. People **were cheering** and the team **was waving** to them. In the office buildings people **were not working**. They **were leaning** out of the windows and **throwing** confetti.

Practice 6.1

Answers (Student's Book page 115)

	SINGULAR		PLURAL	
	Affirmative	**Negative**	**Affirmative**	**Negative**
First person	I was crying	I was not crying	we were crying	we were not crying
Second person	you were crying	you were not crying	you were crying	you were not crying
Third person	he was crying she was crying it was crying	he was not crying she was not crying it was not crying	they were crying	they were not crying

Practice 6.2

Answers (Student's Book pages 115–116)

Going to See the Fireworks

It rained in the afternoon, but by 6:00 P.M. it (not rain) __was not raining__ (1) anymore. There is always a huge crowd for the fireworks, so we had to leave early to get a good spot. At 6:30, we (walk) __were walking__ (2) along the avenue with thousands of other people. Police (guard) __were guarding__ (3) the entrance points and (check) __checking__ (4) people's bags, so the crowd (not move) __was not moving__ (5) very fast. Even so, by 7:00, we (stand) __were standing__ (6) near the river where there was a good view out over the water. It was very crowded, but people (not argue) __were not arguing__ (7) about space. Everyone (make room) __was making room__ (8) for newcomers very cheerfully. Around us, some people (have) __were having__ (9) picnics, while others (sit) __were sitting__ (10) comfortably in folding chairs and (take it easy) __taking it easy__ (11). Four people near us (play) __were playing__ (12) cards. By 8:30, everyone (get) __was getting__ (13) tired of waiting and kids (complain) __were complaining__ (14). It (begin) __was beginning__ (15) to get dark, though. By 9:00, it was dark. Everyone (expect) __was expecting__ (16) the first fireworks to go off at any minute when it finally happened—a dozen big bangs! The rockets whizzed up into the air and burst into fountains of color. Everyone cheered. No one was tired anymore.

EXPLORING THE GRAMMAR POINT

Answers (Student's Book page 116)

In which version did Jiang Zemin and the students cry, stop crying, and then proceed with the speech? *Version 2*

In which version did they cry throughout the beginning of the speech? *Version 1*

Additional examples

1. There was a parade for the soccer team yesterday. People **were cheering** and the team **was waving** to them. In the office buildings, people **were not working**. They **were leaning** out of the windows and **throwing** confetti.

2. There was a parade for the soccer team yesterday. People **cheered** and the team **waved** to them. In the office buildings, people **did not work**. They **leaned** out the windows and **threw** confetti.

Questions and answers for the additional examples

In which version did everything happen at the same time and continue for some time? *Version 1*

In which version did actions happen and then stop? *Version 2*

UNDERSTANDING THE GRAMMAR POINT

Practice 7.1

Answers (Student's Book page 117)

Flying Up

Last Saturday I (volunteer) _____volunteered_____ to take photographs at the

flying-up ceremony for my daughter Julia's Brownie troop. Brownies (be)

_____are_____ little Girl Scouts, six to eight years old. When Brownies (become)

_____become_____ Junior Girl Scouts, it is called "flying up." When we got to the

hall, it (fill up) _____was filling up_____ with people. The flying-up Brownies (stand)

_____were standing_____ together and (act) _____acting_____ very important.

Parents (greet) _____were greeting_____ friends, (look) _____looking_____ for seats,

and (try) _____trying_____ to get their kids' attention. The Brownies' brothers and

sisters (run around) _____were running around_____ and (ignore) _____ignoring_____ their

parents. I (get) _____got_____ some great photos of all the activity.

When the ceremony (start) _____started_____, it was very simple. Each girl
                                    13
(walk) _____walked_____ across the stage, the leader (pin) _____pinned_____
              14   15
a badge to her uniform, everyone (clap) _____clapped_____, and the girl (walk off)
                                              16
_____walked off_____ the other side of the stage. I took some photos of the girls while
          17
they (wait) _____were waiting_____ in line, and then I (take) _____took_____ one
                      18   19
of each girl as she (receive) _____received_____ her wings. The next day I (put)
                                        20
_____put_____ the best photos on the troop's Web site for everyone to see.
      21

Grammar Point 8 ## Stative Verbs

This grammar point reiterates the guideline that stative verbs cannot be used in progressive
tenses. This is covered in more detail in *Chapter 6,* Grammar Point 10 (page 98).

EXPLORING THE GRAMMAR POINT

Additional examples (Student's Book page 118)

- **Incorrect:** I bought a muffin. It **was costing** three dollars. It **wasn't containing** any sugar
  or fat.
  Correct: I bought a muffin. It **cost** three dollars. It **didn't contain** any sugar or fat.

UNDERSTANDING THE GRAMMAR POINT

Practice 8.1

All the sentences are about birthdays, but they are not connected in a narrative.

Answers (Student's Book page 118)

1. Little Evelyn (look) ___looked___ absolutely beautiful. She (wear) **was wearing** the
   outfit we gave her for her birthday last month.

2. For weeks before Ricky's birthday, I (try) **was trying** to think of something fun for
   the party. When someone (suggest) **suggested** a roller skating party, it (sound)
   ___sounded___ like a good idea.

3. The birthday cake (be) ___was___ three feet tall, (weigh) ___weighed___ fifty pounds,
   and (cost) ___cost___ more than $500.

4. While the guests (arrive) **were arriving**, I (watch) **was watching** Eddie. He (feel)
   was feeling the presents, (shake) ___shaking___ them, and (weigh) ___weighing___ them
   in his hands to try to guess what they were.

5. I (forget) ___forgot___ Paul's birthday last year. Three days later, when I (remember)
   remembered it, I (look) ___looked___ at my date book. I (feel) ___felt___ terrible.

6. On my mother's birthday last year, we (have) ___had___ a party for her. We (not
   have) **did not have** enough chairs, so some people (sit) ___sat___ on the floor.

CHAPTER 7 REVIEW

Review Practice 7.1

Answers (Student's Book page 120)

The Joy of Country Life

When I was eight years old, my parents ~~were taking~~ *took* a trip with me and my sister to

my uncle's house in the country. This was my first opportunity to enjoy rural life. There

~~was being~~ *was* no pleasure greater than being able to enjoy the refreshing country air in the

middle of the summer along with the discovery of so many kinds of wildlife. In the late

afternoons, my sister and I ~~enjoy~~ *enjoyed* the cool breezes while we ~~run~~ *ran* and laughed and ~~catch~~ *caught*

insects. We also ~~see~~ *saw* many new kinds of beautiful birds, but we didn't ~~caught~~ *catch* any. One

day we ~~going~~ *went* fishing in the lake with my uncle. This was our first time, so our uncle

~~teached~~ *taught* us how to do it. The fish were ~~bite~~ *biting* very well that summer, and we ~~catch~~ *caught* twenty

fish in three hours. This really ~~add~~ *added* to my joy. Because of this wonderful experience filled

with many new discoveries for me, my opinion about the country ~~change~~ *changed*. Now I firmly

believe that the country is a much more enjoyable place for a vacation than the city.

Review Practice 7.2

Answers (Student's Book pages 120–121)

Jumping the Broom

I went to Tanika's wedding last week. While everybody ~~was arrive~~ *was arriving*, I ~~run~~ *ran* into Professor

Gold. And then in the church, while we ~~waiting~~ *were waiting* for the ceremony to start, I saw lots of

other people I knew. Well, the music was good, Tanika ~~look~~ *looked* stunning, and her husband

~~seem~~ *seemed* like a nice guy. I thought the ceremony was over when the maid of honor ~~walk~~ *walked* to

the front of the church. She ~~is carrying~~ *was carrying* a broom. It ~~look~~ *looked* like an ordinary broom except

that it had ribbons on it. I ~~try~~ *was trying* to figure out what was happening when Tanika's father

~~come~~ *came* up to the front and ~~spoked~~ *spoke* about what the broom represents. Apparently it's an

African-American custom from the days of slavery. Slaves were not allowed to marry,

developed
so they ~~develop~~ a way of marrying themselves. The couple ~~bring~~ their friends together,
brought
laid
promised to love each other, and then ~~lay~~ a broom on the floor and jumped over it. It
meant
~~meaned~~ that they were married. And Tanika and her husband ~~do~~ just that. The maid of
did
put   *held*   *counted*
honor ~~putting~~ the broom on the floor, they ~~hold~~ hands, everyone ~~count~~ 1-2-3, and they
are jumping / jump
jumped over the broom! Now I understand that many African-American couples ~~jumping~~
felt
the broom at their weddings these days. I ~~was felt~~ really ignorant because I had never

heard of this custom before.

Review Practice 7.3

Answers (Student's Book pages 121–122)

Elizabeth Blackwell's Graduation

took place
The commencement ceremony ~~was taking place~~ on a Tuesday morning in January.
arrived
The sun was shining brightly. We ~~were arriving~~ an hour early, but the seats were filling
did not get   *appeared*
up already, and we ~~were not getting~~ a seat in front. It ~~was appearing~~ that most of the
saw
spectators were women. From the gallery, we ~~were seeing~~ a sea of bonnets. At about
entered
eleven o'clock, Miss Blackwell ~~was entering~~ with the other medical students. She was

wearing a black silk dress with a lace collar, but she wasn't wearing a hat or shawl.
got
There was some music before the students ~~were getting~~ their diplomas. While the

choir was singing, Miss Blackwell sat on the side with old Mrs. Waller. After the music,
called
President Hale ~~was calling~~ the graduates to go up and receive their diplomas. He was

speaking Latin and I saw that he was reading the words from a piece of paper! Of
came
course, everyone was waiting for Miss Blackwell, and she ~~was coming~~ last. While she
spoke   *gave*
was climbing the steps, Dr. Hale stood up to meet her. He ~~was speaking~~ and ~~giving~~ her
bowed   *appeared*
the diploma, and ~~bowing~~. Then he ~~was appearing~~ to expect her to leave. Not so! She
seemed
~~was seeming~~ embarrassed, but she was struggling to speak. After a moment, she ~~was~~
thanked
~~thanking~~ him. She said that she hoped to "shed honor on this diploma." Then she ~~was~~

~~going~~ **went** to sit among the graduates. Everyone ~~was applauding~~ **applauded** enthusiastically. Miss B.

was blushing, but she ~~was becoming~~ **became** calm again while the next speaker, Dr. Lee, was

speaking. The program ~~was being~~ **was** over soon. While people were leaving, many of them

~~were stopping~~ **stopped** to congratulate Miss Blackwell. Finally, she ~~was standing up~~ **stood up**, ~~putting~~ **put on**

~~on~~ her hat and shawl, ~~taking~~ **took** the arm of her brother (who came from New York to be

present), and ~~leaving~~ **left** the first woman M.D.!

The Present Perfect and the Present Perfect Progressive

In the United States, even in educated speech and academic writing, it is quite common to use the simple past tense in some contexts where the present perfect (for unspecified past time) can also be used. In the interest of simplicity, *Nitty Gritty Grammar* does not discuss this dual usage. However, you may wish to acknowledge it in your lessons on the present perfect.

EXPLORING THE TOPIC

The passage "Fighting for Donny Ray" is from *The Rainmaker* by John Grisham. Grisham is an American lawyer and writer who specializes in "legal thrillers"—crime fiction about lawyers and the law. He writes approximately one novel a year, all of which have become best sellers. Many of his books have been made into movies, including *The Firm, The Pelican Brief, The Client,* and *The Rainmaker.*

Answers (Student's Book page 124)

In *Chapters 6* and *7,* students saw that progressive tenses have *-ing* endings. They should be able to infer that the two verbs with *-ing, have been calling* and *has been sitting,* are examples of the present perfect progressive tense. Therefore, the seven other italicized verbs are in the present perfect.

Grammar Point 1 ▶ The Form of the Present Perfect

If you wish, you can use the additional examples below to teach the three pronunciations of the *-d* / *-ed* ending of regular past participles: /əd/, /d/, and /t/.

EXPLORING THE GRAMMAR POINT

Additional examples (Student's Book page 124)

- The swimming pool at the club **has needed** repairs for years.
- Now they **have emptied** the pool.
- They **have fixed** it.
- They **haven't filled** it again.

UNDERSTANDING THE GRAMMAR POINT

Additional examples of regular verbs (Student's Book page 125)

Base form	Past tense	Past participle
like	liked	liked
travel	traveled	traveled
marry	married	married
want	wanted	wanted

In affirmative sentences, contract *have* and *has* with pronoun subjects. In negatives, contract *have* and *has* with *not*.

Additional examples of contractions with *have* and *has*

- **They've** spent a lot of time together.
- She **hasn't** agreed to marry him.

Practice 1.1

Answers (Student's Book page 125)

THE PRESENT PERFECT		
	Singular	**Plural**
First person	I have started I have not started	we have started we have not started
Second person	you have started you have not started	you have started you have not started
Third person	he has started he has not started she has started she has not started it has started it has not started	they have started they have not started

---

Grammar Point 2 | **Irregular Verbs in the Present Perfect Tense**

UNDERSTANDING THE GRAMMAR POINT

Additional examples of irregular verbs with the same form for past tense and past participle (Student's Book page 126)

Base form	Past tense	Past participle
cost	cost	cost
say	said	said
win	won	won

Additional examples of irregular verbs with different forms for past tense and past participle

Base form	Past tense	Past participle
come	came	come
forget	forgot	forgotten
know	knew	known

Practice 2.1

The passage, in the form of a log or diary, illustrates the use of the present perfect for unspecified past time. The events happened at unspecified points in time before the date of each entry in the log. This use of the present perfect is introduced in Grammar Point 3.

Additional information about mediation

Mediation is becoming more and more common in the United States. It is different from arbitration. In arbitration, typically the parties make their cases to the arbitrator and must then accept his or her decision. In mediation, the mediator helps the parties reach an agreement that all contribute to and all can accept. Sometimes mediation is ordered by a judge to try to avoid a trial. At other times the parties seek mediation privately. Mediation is common in situations such as labor disputes, divorce, and child custody, and also in disagreements between neighbors, tenants and landlords, parents and schools, and so on.

Answers (Student's Book pages 126–127)

August 10: The Problem

Connie Wu (want) _____has wanted_____ to remodel her kitchen for a long time. She
                              1

(hire) _____has hired_____ Bob Schaeffer, a contractor, to do the work. Bob (buy)
                    2

_____has bought_____ all the materials and (begin) _____begun_____ the work.
            3   4

However, Connie (not pay) _____has not paid_____ him for the materials yet. As a result,
                                            5

Bob (stop) _____has stopped_____ working on the kitchen.
                        6

August 24: The Mediation

Connie and Bob (take) _____have taken_____ their disagreement to a mediator. In
                                      7

conversations with the mediator, Bob (come) _____has come_____ to understand
                                                            8

that Connie is afraid he will never finish the work if she pays him now. Connie (realize)

_____has realized_____ that Bob has a right to be paid for the materials.
            9

August 30: The Result

Bob (give) _____has given_____ Connie letters from several satisfied customers, so
                        10

Connie now feels more confident about Bob. Connie (pay) _____has paid_____ Bob
                                                                              11

for the materials, and Bob (start) _____has started_____ to work on the kitchen again.
                                                12

The Present Perfect for Unspecified Past Time

EXPLORING THE GRAMMAR POINT

Additional examples (Student's Book page 127)

• We **have read** the book.
• Josh **has seen** the movie four times.

UNDERSTANDING THE GRAMMAR POINT

Additional examples
• **Correct:**   We **have read** the book.
• **Correct:**   We **read** the book last year.
   Incorrect: We **have read** the book last year.

Practice 3.1

Additional information about expert witnesses

The text describes the roles of psychologists and psychiatrists who give testimony about psychological issues in court cases. They testify for one side in the case and are paid for their testimony, which must be true and unbiased.

Answers (Student's Book page 128)

Psychologists and Psychiatrists As Expert Witnesses

Both psychologists and psychiatrists often serve as experts in trials. "Expert testimony"

(become) ___has become___ very common in both civil and criminal trials. However,
                    1

the training of psychologists and psychiatrists is quite different. Psychologists' training

is specifically in the field of psychology. A psychologist (attend) ___has attended___
                                                                                2

graduate school in psychology and (complete) ___completed___ his or her
                                                          3

training in a clinic or counseling office. Psychologists cannot prescribe drugs for their

patients. Psychiatrists, on the other hand, have medical training. Psychiatrists (attend)

___have attended___ medical school and (obtain) ___obtained___ the M.D.
          4   5

(doctor of medicine) degree. They (complete) ___have completed___ a training period
                                                              6

in a hospital. Due to these differences in training, psychiatrists usually charge more as

expert witnesses than psychologists do.

Frequency Adverbs with the Present Perfect

This grammar point assumes that students have already learned the meaning of basic frequency adverbs. You may wish to review their meanings if your students are unsure of them. There is a list of common frequency adverbs on page 93 of the Student's Book.

UNDERSTANDING THE GRAMMAR POINT

Additional examples (Student's Book page 128)
- We have **always** lived in the city.
- The country has **never** attracted us.
- No small town has **ever** tempted us to move.

Practice 4.1

Answers (Student's Book page 129)

A Prison in Japan

There (never be) ___has never been___ a hostage crisis in the prison. There
                           1

(never be) ___has never been___ a "prison disturbance." Gang wars (never occur)
                 2

___have never occurred___ there—in fact, no gangs (ever exist) ___have ever existed___
        3   4

in the prison. No prisoner (ever kill) ___has ever killed___ a guard or another
                                              5

prisoner. Only three prisoners (try) ___have tried___ to escape in the last ten
                                            6

years. Guards in all Japanese prisons are highly trained. Last year, two-thirds of the

applicants who (pass) ___passed___ the national test for prison guards (be)
                           7

___were___ university graduates. Even so, only one quarter of them (get)
        8

___have gotten / got___ jobs as prison guards.
        9

The Present Perfect for Past to Present Time (and Possibly the Future)

EXPLORING THE GRAMMAR POINT

Answers (Student's Book page 129)

Did these actions begin in the past or in the present? *In the past*

Did they end in the past or are they still continuing? *The actions are still continuing.*

Additional examples (Student's Book page 129)
- Erica **has known** Ralph for about three years.
- She and Ralph **have liked** each other since they met.

UNDERSTANDING THE GRAMMAR POINT

Additional examples (Student's Book page 130)

* **Incorrect:** They **áre** married for a month.
  Correct: They **have been** married for a month.
* **Incorrect:** Ralph and Erica **worked** in the same place since May.
  Correct: Ralph and Erica **have worked** in the same place since May.

| Grammar Point 6 | *For* and *Since* with the Present Perfect |

UNDERSTANDING THE GRAMMAR POINT

Additional examples

For

* Tim has been a high-school teacher **for 12 years**.

Since

* Laura has had her car **since last September**.

Since with a clause

* Colin and Judy have lived next door **since I started school**.

Practice 6.1

Answers (Student's Book page 130)

1. Amy has been with her father in Canada _____**for**_____ three years.
2. She has not seen her mother in China _____**since**_____ 2002.
3. Her parents have lived in separate countries _____**for**_____ twenty years.
4. Amy's father has sent money home every month _____**since**_____ he arrived in Canada.
5. Amy's mother has raised their children alone _____**for**_____ most of their lives.
6. Amy has felt homesick _____**since**_____ she came to Canada.

Practice 6.2

Answers (Student's Book page 131)

	1974	1987	1989	1990	1992	1997	1998	2001	NOW
1. be in the U.S.									→
2. have his own business									→
3. know his wife									→
4. belong to the gym									→
5. be married									→
6. vote every year									→
7. live in his present house									→
8. have his Corvette									→

Answers for 4, 5, and 8

4. He has belonged to the gym since 1989.

5. He has been married since 1992.

8. He has had his Corvette since 1997.

Answers for 2, 3, 6, and 7. Answers will vary depending on the year when the students are writing.

2. He has had his own business for (X) years.

3. He has known his wife for (X) years.

6. He has voted every year for (X) years.

7. He has lived in his present house for (X) years.

Practice 6.3

Answers (Student's Book page 132)

1. According to the New York City Police Department, the city (lead) __has led__ the U.S. in fighting crime since 1990.

2. The crime rate (fall) __fell__ 6 percent last year.

3. Last year, there (be) __were__ only about 230,000 crimes of all kinds in the city.

4. In 1990, the number of crimes (be) __was__ more than 700,000.

5. The city's murder rate (go down) __has gone down__ for the last sixteen years.

6. New York (have) __has had__ fewer murders during the last two years than at any time since the early 1960s.

7. For the last two years, New York (rank) __has ranked__ number one for safety among big cities in the country.

8. In fact, last year, New York (be) __was__ safer than some American cities with only 100,000 people.

Grammar Point 7 ▶ The Form of the Present Perfect Progressive

---

EXPLORING THE GRAMMAR POINT

Additional examples (Student's Book page 132)

• She**'s been waiting** here for an hour.

• It **has been raining** the whole time.

UNDERSTANDING THE GRAMMAR POINT

Additional examples

• Marc **has not been feeling** well today. / Marc **hasn't been feeling** well today.

• His headache **has not been getting** better. / His headache **hasn't been getting** better.

• He **has been taking** aspirin. / He**'s been taking** aspirin.

Practice 7.1
Answers (Student's Book page 133)

THE PRESENT PERFECT PROGRESSIVE		
	Singular	**Plural**
First person	I have been waiting I have not been waiting	we have been waiting we have not been waiting
Second person	you have been waiting you have not been waiting	you have been waiting you have not been waiting
Third person	he has been waiting he has not been waiting she has been waiting she has not been waiting it has been waiting it has not been waiting	they have been waiting they have not been waiting

Grammar Point 8 Stative Verbs

EXPLORING THE GRAMMAR POINT
Additional examples (Student's Book page 133)
- **Correct:** They **have been sitting** in class.
- **Incorrect:** They **have been being** in class.

UNDERSTANDING THE GRAMMAR POINT
This grammar point assumes that students already know what stative verbs are, so you may wish to review if your students are unsure of them. Stative verbs describe a state or condition rather than an action. There is a list of common stative verbs on page 99 of the Student's Book.

Practice 8.1
Answers (Student's Book page 134)

1. Ana (practice) __has been practicing__ the piano for an hour.
2. I (listen) __have been listening__ to my phone messages. There's one from Leo.
3. She (own) __has owned__ that car for five years.
4. I (not have) __have not had__ a bad headache all year.
5. Li (think) __has been thinking__ about going back to school.
6. Rex (try) __has been trying__ to get away for a vacation, but he's too busy.
7. Jack (weigh) __has weighed__ exactly the same since he was in high school.
8. It's so nice to meet you! Niki (tell) __has been telling__ me all about you.

9. In the last thirty years, the diamond (belong to) __has belonged to__ three princes and an actress.

10. We (love) _____have loved_____ each other since we were children.

Grammar Point 9 · The Present Perfect Progressive for Emphasizing Duration

EXPLORING THE GRAMMAR POINT

Additional examples (Student's Book page 134)

• She**'s been fixing** her bike all afternoon.
  She**'s fixed** her bike all afternoon.

• It **has been snowing** every day this winter.
  It **has snowed** every day this winter.

UNDERSTANDING THE GRAMMAR POINT

Remind students that *for* is followed by a time phrase, whereas *since* can be followed by a time phrase or a clause.

Additional examples

• Teddy has been sitting in the cafe **since ten o'clock / since he was fired this morning**.
• He's been drinking coffee **for hours**.

Practice 9.1

Students' answers will vary.

Suggested answers (Student's Book page 135)

1. The car alarm has been going off for over an hour.
2. She has been waiting for the bus for a long time.
3. The kids have been watching TV since they got home from school.
4. Mr. Ford has been stealing money from the company for years.
5. Carlos has been looking for a job for months.
6. Some kids at Grady's school have been teasing him and stealing his things since he started going there.

Practice 9.2

Answers (Student's Book page 136)

1. I (do) __have been doing__ my homework for three hours. I'm sick of it.

2. I (do) _____have done_____ my homework. Let's go to the movies.

3. We (paint) __have painted__ the house. Now we can move in.

4. We (paint) __have been painting__ the house all day.

5. Rod (never play) __has never played__ tennis.

6. Su Ling (play) _____has played_____ tennis two or three times.

7. Roger and Carl (play) __have been playing__ tennis since breakfast.

8. Rachel (write) __has been writing__ poetry since she was twelve.

9. Many people (write) __have written__ a poem at some time in their lives.

10. Most people (not write) __have not written__ a good poem.

11. I (eat) __have eaten__ some very strange things in different places around the world.

12. They (eat and talk) __have been eating and talking__ for three hours.

CHAPTER 8 REVIEW

Review Practice 8.1

Answers (Student's Book page 138)

1. Does Jack live in Ottawa? Yes. *(He has lived there from two years ago until now, and he will probably continue to live there in the future.)*

2. What is already typed? *His English term paper.* *(He typed it at some indefinite time in the past.)*

3. What is not completely typed yet? *His history term paper.* *(He is still typing it.)*

4. Is Jack still reading the books? *No.* *(He finished reading them at some indefinite time in the past.)*

Additional questions and answers about the statements in the Student's Book

• When did Jack get his laptop? *Last week. / A week ago.*

• Does Jack live in Canada? *Yes. (He moved there ten years ago.)*

MEANING		PRESENT PERFECT	PRESENT PERFECT PROGRESSIVE
Unspecified Past Time		(1) Jack has typed his English term paper. Jack has read several books for his term paper.	(2) *There is no sentence for this box.* Explanation (probably best not conveyed to your students): *Nitty Gritty Grammar* does not teach this less common use of the present perfect progressive tense, which describes activities or situations that ended at the moment of speaking / writing or in the very recent past. Examples would be: • I've **been waiting** to see you. • Joe **has just been telling** us about his trip.
Past to Present Time	Active verbs	(3) Jack has lived in Canada for ten years.	(4) Jack has been typing his history term paper. Jack has been living in Ottawa for two years.
	Stative verbs	(5) Jack has had his laptop since last week.	(6) *There is no sentence for this box.* Explanation: Progressive tenses are generally not used with stative verbs.

Review Practice 8.2

In this review practice exercise, some problems with the perfect tenses also involve the simple past tense.

Answers (Student's Book page 139)

The Courtship of Sue and Joe

Things have been getting serious between Sue and Joe recently. Sue has lived in

Miami ~~since~~ *for* over four years. She and Joe ~~have been knowing~~ *have known* each other for almost two

years. They have taken several classes together at Miami Dade Community College. Last

year they ~~have taken~~ *took* two English classes together, and they ~~have started~~ *started* dating regularly

about six months ago. They ~~didn't date~~ *haven't dated* anyone else since then. Lately, they have been

talking about getting married.

Review Practice 8.3

In this review practice, some problems with the perfect tenses also involve the simple past tense.

Answers (Student's Book page 139)

A Problem at School

Someone has defined bullying as "doing something to hurt another person or cause

him stress." At my daughter's school, bullying ~~has been increase~~ *has been increasing* for the last two years.

Bullying ~~always been~~ *has always been* a problem among schoolchildren. However, the bullies have usually

been boys, not girls. A couple of months ago, I ~~have seen~~ *saw* two older girls who were

bullying a younger girl at my daughter's school. They ~~have pushed~~ *pushed* her down, took her

backpack, and threw it into a busy street. When I got out of my car to help the girl, the

bullies ~~have run~~ *ran* away.

Recently, my daughter ~~acts~~ *has been acting* strangely. She doesn't want to go to school, and I am

afraid someone is bullying her. I am trying to get her to talk about it, but she refuses to

discuss it. This morning she ~~has said~~ *said* she was sick and I let her stay home. But I ~~have~~

~~been deciding~~ *have decided* it's time to get tough. We have to talk.

Review Practice 8.4

In this review practice, some problems with the perfect tenses also involve the simple past tense.

The passage "Transit Blues" is true. Darius McCollum is a real person. His story was widely reported a few years ago.

Answers (Student's Book page 140)

Transit Blues

Darius McCollum, 39, has spent more than a third of his life in jail. New York City

police ~~arrest~~ *have arrested* him more than twenty times for pretending to be a transit worker. He

~~drive~~ *has driven* buses and subway trains. He ~~operate~~ *has operated* signals and switches. He has done almost

everything that transit workers do, but he has never worked for the Metropolitan Transit

Authority. Time after time, McCollum ~~is~~ *has been* able to acquire official MTA keys, tools, uniforms,

and documents. He has just spent three and a half years in prison for pretending to be a

transit supervisor and stopping a subway train.

When McCollum was eight, he ~~know~~ *knew* the entire New York City subway system.

Although it is a large and complex system, the boy ~~is~~ *was* able to give directions from any

station to any other station from memory. Some medical experts ~~have suggest~~ *have suggested* that

McCollum has a condition called Asperger's syndrome. People with Asperger's syndrome

often become incredibly expert about specific topics and talk about them endlessly. Many

of them do not have good social skills and are not able to hold a job. Recently, McCollum

~~is attending~~ *has been attending* an Asperger's support group. He and his wife ~~are living~~ *have been living* in Manhattan since

he left jail. They met on the subway.

The Future

English does not have a "future tense" in the same way that it has past, present, progressive, and perfect tenses. Students may believe that *will* always expresses future time, and that *will* is the most common way to express future time in English. Actually, *be going to* is the most common way to express future time in English. *Will* expresses meanings other than a future time frame, although these other uses are not discussed in this chapter. Examples of other uses of *will* are making promises (*I'll never do it again*) and expressing immediate intention (*Someone's at the door. I'll get it.*).

EXPLORING THE TOPIC

The passage "New Home Safety Product from Ogata Robotics" was written for *Nitty Gritty Grammar* in the style of a corporate news release. The Guard Puppy has features in common with several actual robotic products, but it does not exist.

Answers to the tasks and the question (verbs that refer to a time in the future are in boldface) (Student's Book pages 141–142)

New Home Safety Product from Ogata Robotics

Ogata Robotics has announced plans for a new home-safety robot, the Guard Puppy.

The new robot **will sense** intruders or fire. It **will automatically call** police or firefighters. It **will also detect** medical emergencies and **call** for assistance.

Ogata Robotics Vice President for Marketing Miharu Tanaka says, "We are designing the Guard Puppy especially for people who are away all day and for elderly people living alone. It **is going to be** very easy to operate and very cute. It **will actually look** like a puppy."

When **will** the Guard Puppy **reach** consumers? "We**'re introducing** it next April," says Ogata. "It **comes out** first in Japan, and we**'re taking** it to the U.S. and Europe in the fall."

EXPLORING THE GRAMMAR POINT

Answer (Student's Book page 142)

The form of *be* is *is* or *are*, depending on the subject. The form of *will* does not change. (*Will* is a true modal like *should* or *may*, and has only one form. *Be going to* is a phrasal modal like *have to*, and it changes to agree with the subject. See *Chapter 10, Modals,* for more about modals.)

Additional examples (Student's Book page 142)

• The deserts out West **are going to bloom** next month.
• We **are going to drive** to California to see the beautiful cactus flowers.
• We **will be** there for a week.
• It **will be** a lot of fun.

UNDERSTANDING THE GRAMMAR POINT

Additional information about contractions (Student's Book page 142)

Both *be going to* and *will* are usually contracted in speech, and often in writing as well. Full forms are expected in academic writing, but contractions are sometimes preferred in other kinds of writing. In less formal writing, both *am / is / are* and *will* are often contracted with subject pronouns and *not* (the contraction of *will not* is *won't*).

• **I'm** going to buy this.
• **She's** going to be late.
• We **aren't** going to take a vacation.
• **They'll** take the bus.
• I hope it **won't** rain.

Practice 1.1

You may wish to ask students for both full forms and contractions (items 1, 3, and 8). There are no negatives in this exercise.

Answers (Student's Book pages 142–143)

1. (it / rain) __It is / It's going to rain__ before we get home.
2. (Ed and I / meet) __Ed and I are going to meet__ after work.
3. (I / start) __I am / I'm going to start__ college in August.
4. (Luisa / buy) __Luisa is going to buy__ a car as soon as she gets a job.
5. (my brother / call) __My brother is going to call__ me from the airport.
6. (my neighbors / install) __My neighbors are going to install__ a security system before they leave on vacation.
7. (older people / like) __Older people will like__ the new product.
8. (I / e-mail) __I will / I'll e-mail__ you when I get there.
9. (my assistant / fax) __My assistant will fax__ the information to you.
10. (the office / close) __The office will close__ at 1:00 tomorrow.

The Form of Future Time Clauses

EXPLORING THE GRAMMAR POINT

The time subordinators (referred to in the footnote on Student's Book page 143) are illustrated on page 25 of the Student's Book in a past time frame, but most of them can also be used for future time.

Additional examples (Student's Book page 143)
- I am going to save **until I have enough to buy an apartment**.
- **After I get home**, I'll make some phone calls.
- I won't see you again **before I leave**.

UNDERSTANDING THE GRAMMAR POINT

Additional examples (Student's Book page 143)
- **Correct:** I'm not going to take a break until I **finish** this.
- **Incorrect:** I'm not going to take a break until I **will finish** this.

Practice 2.1

Answers (Student's Book page 144)

1. I'm going to take a road trip ___as soon as my vacation starts___ .
2. I won't be able to leave ___until I finish___ this big project at work.
3. I'll have to make my plans for the trip ___before I finish / while I am finishing___ the project.
4. I'm going to take this trip ___while I have___ the money.
5. ___Before my trip is over___ , I'm going to ride every roller coaster between here and Orlando.
6. The new roller coaster at Six Flags in New Jersey will be open ___by the time / before I get there___ .
7. I'm going to take a lot of photographs ___while I'm traveling___ .
8. I'll show you my photographs ___after / as soon as I get home___ .

Predictions with *Be Going To* and *Will*

UNDERSTANDING THE GRAMMAR POINT

Additional examples (Student's Book page 145)
- The movie **will be over** at 9:20.
  The movie **is going to be over** at 9:20.
- Techline **will introduce** a new model next year.
  Techline **is going to introduce** a new model next year.

Additional examples (only *be going to* can be used)
- **Correct:** I just wrecked my sister's car. She**'s going to be** angry.
  Incorrect: I just wrecked my sister's car. She **will be** angry.

Practice 3.1

Answers (Student's Book page 145)

1. My daughter is going to be in second grade next year.
   My daughter will be in second grade next year.
2. Things will get worse before they get better.
   Things are going to get worse before they get better.
3. He's going to pass this time.
4. We're going to be late.
5. There's going to be a reception after the ceremony.
   There will be a reception after the ceremony.
6. I'm sure they're going to be very happy.
   I'm sure they will be very happy.

| Grammar Point 4 | Plans and Intentions with *Be Going To* and the Present Progressive |

EXPLORING THE GRAMMAR POINT

Answers (Student's Book page 146)

Which sentence expresses an intention or indefinite plan?   *Sentence 1*

Which sentences express definite plans?   *Sentences 2 and 3*

Which sentence does not express a future meaning?   *Sentence 4*

Additional examples
- One of these days Rob **is going to sail** around the world.
- Rob **is going to sail** around the world as soon as he retires.
- Rob **is sailing** around the world as soon as he retires.
- Rob **is sailing** around the world. Right now he's near Hawaii.

UNDERSTANDING THE GRAMMAR POINT

Practice 4.1

Students should write about their own real plans and intentions in order to refine their understanding of the two future forms. Their answers in 1 should use *be going to*; their answers in 2 can use either *be going to* or the present progressive.

Students might discuss their ideas in pairs before writing their sentences. They should question each other until they are confident that each of them is expressing plans that really are indefinite or definite, as required. Encourage them to use appropriate future time markers, including time clauses. Their answers will vary.

Scheduled and Planned Events with the Simple Present and the Present Progressive

EXPLORING THE GRAMMAR POINT

Answers (Student's Book page 147)

Which sentences are about scheduled events that cannot change? *Sentences 2, 3, and 5*

What verb tense do they use? *The simple present tense*

Which are about personal plans that probably will not change? *Sentences 1 and 4*

What tense do they use? *The present progressive*

Additional examples
- Joann **is seeing*** a play with Alan tonight.
- The curtain **goes up** at 8:00.
- The show **lasts** until 10:30.
- She**'s taking** the train home.
- Her train **leaves** at 11:20.

*Notice that *see* has an active meaning here, although it is often a stative verb.

Practice 5.1

Answers (Student's Book page 147)

1. Tomorrow we (get to) _____**are getting to**_____ Yellowstone National Park sometime before lunch.

2. We (take) _____**are taking**_____ a picnic and (eat) _____**eating**_____ in the park.

3. We (stay) _____**are staying**_____ at a hotel inside the park.

4. There (be) _____**is**_____ a fireworks show at the hotel tomorrow night.

5. The sun (set) _____**sets**_____ at 8:30 tomorrow, and the fireworks (start) _____**start**_____ at 9:00.

6. We (have) _____**are having**_____ dinner at the hotel before the fireworks.

7. They (show) _____**are showing**_____ *Casablanca* after the fireworks.

8. It (not be) _____**isn't**_____ over until 11:30, but we (go) _____**are going**_____ anyway. We love that movie.

Future Forms in Longer Passages

This grammar point focuses on written discourse. Developing writers sometimes overuse *be going to* in written work that is personal or somewhat informal (even if written for an academic purpose). Also, they may not be aware that *will* is the usual future form in formal writing.

EXPLORING THE GRAMMAR POINT

Additional examples (Student's Book page 148)

Passage 1 (From personal correspondence)

Liz **is going to spend** the summer in the U.S. She**'s leaving** Yola on Saturday and **flying** to Abuja. She**'ll spend** the night in Abuja and **leave** early Sunday morning. She **arrives** in Boston Sunday night. I expect she**'ll call** me on Monday.

Passage 2 (From a company memo)

The company picnic **will take place** on Friday, July 8, this year. The office **will close** at noon so that everyone can attend. Buses **will provide** transportation to the park for those who do not wish to drive. They **will return** to the park at 5:00, and **make** stops at the office and the train station.

Practice 6.1

Students are required to choose an appropriate future form based on the first guideline given in Grammar Point 6: Informal writing often begins with *be going to*, then continues with shorter future forms.

Note that some of the choices are perhaps more subtle than the guideline implies. In several places, the present progressive sounds unnatural, although the guideline allows it. It is likely that your students will not be able to make this judgment. Reassure them that these guidelines are, after all, "the nitty gritty," and that with experience, their choices will become more accurate.

Although both *will* and the present progressive are given as answers in most cases, the passage will be more natural if there is a mix of the two forms, not just one or the other.

Answers (Student's Book page 149)

I'm going to spend the day with my two little nieces tomorrow. Before I go, I'm going [~~'ll make / 'm making~~] to make a picnic. I'm going to take [~~'m taking / 'll take~~] my bicycle with me, and when I pick them up, I'm going to put [~~'ll~~] their bikes in my car [*put (but not I'm putting)*]. First, I'm going to take [~~'ll take / 'm taking~~] them to the park, and we're going to ride [~~'ll~~] our bikes for a while [*ride (but not we're riding)*]. Then we're going to find [~~'ll find (but not I'm finding)~~] a nice place and have our picnic. After lunch, I'm going to take [~~'m taking / 'll take~~] them to the movies. It's going to be a great day.

Practice 6.2

Students must apply the second guideline in Grammar Practice 6. All instances of *be going to* should be changed to *will*, although the first one (the example) could be left as *are going to see*.

Answers (Student's Book page 149)

Hotels of the Future

In the future, we ~~are going to~~ _will_ see hotels in places we can hardly imagine today.

Next year, an undersea hotel ~~is going to open~~ _will open_ in Dubai. Plans already exist for portable

hotels, carried by helicopter. They ~~are going to appear~~ _will appear_ almost overnight in the desert,

on mountaintops, or in the rainforest. They ~~are going to be~~ _will be_ self-contained and safe for

the environment. Soon, too, travelers ~~are going to find~~ _will find_ hotels in space. Some ~~are going~~

~~to be~~ _will be_ in orbit around the Earth. Others ~~are going to rise~~ _will rise_ on the surface of the Moon, or

even Mars.

Future in the past may not seem to qualify as part of the "nitty gritty" of grammar. It is introduced because it often comes up in student writing, and its form can be taught in very simple terms.

Grammar Point 7 ▷ **Meaning**

EXPLORING THE GRAMMAR POINT

Additional examples (Student's Book pages 149–150)

Passage 1

Liz **is going to spend** the summer in the U.S. She**'s leaving** Yola on Saturday and **flying** to Abuja. She**'ll spend** the night in Abuja and **leave** early Sunday morning. She**'s arriving** in Boston Sunday night. I expect she**'ll call** me on Monday.

Passage 2

Liz **was going to spend** that summer in the U.S. She **was leaving** Yola on Saturday and **flying** to Abuja. She **would spend** the night in Abuja and **leave** early Sunday morning. She **was arriving** in Boston Sunday night. I expected she **would call** me on Monday.

Grammar Point 8 ▷ **Form**

This grammar point explains the formation of future in the past verb phrases in simple, mechanical terms, without referring to the past perfect tense (which is not taught in _Nitty Gritty Grammar_).

EXPLORING THE GRAMMAR POINT

Answers (Student's Book page 150)

PASSAGE 1	PASSAGE 2
will do	would do
am/is/are going to do	was / were going to do
am/is/are doing	was / were doing

UNDERSTANDING THE GRAMMAR POINT

Additional examples (Student's Book page 151)

• She **would spend** the night in Abuja.
• She **was going to spend** the night in Abuja.

Practice 8.1

Answers (Student's Book page 151)

American Pie

It ~~is~~ [was] 2002 and Pascale Le Draoulec ~~is going to move~~ [was going to move] from California to New York. She ~~is going to be~~ [was going to be] a restaurant critic for the *New York Daily News*. She ~~is driving~~ [was driving] across the country with a friend, a photographer. They ~~are going to look for~~ [were going to look for] pie and pie bakers all across the United States. The trip ~~will be~~ [would be / was going to be] a long one because Pascale ~~is going to write~~ [was going to write] a book about it. She ~~believes~~ [believed] that people ~~will talk~~ [would talk] freely to her about pie and about their lives. She ~~hopes~~ [hoped] they ~~will invite~~ [would invite] her into their homes and share their recipes with her. She ~~knows~~ [knew] she ~~will find~~ [would find / was going to find] both good pie and bad pie, but she ~~is~~ [was] sure it ~~will be~~ [would be] a good trip.

Practice 8.2

Answers (Student's Book page 152)

In the fall ~~I'm going to explore~~ [he was going to explore his] ~~my~~ own country. ~~I'm buying~~ [He was buying / He would buy] a pick-up truck with a camper on the back. ~~I'm traveling~~ [He was traveling / He would travel] alone except for Charley. ~~I'll start~~ [He would start / He was starting] in the east and ~~drive~~ [drive / driving] northwest, zigzagging through the mid-western states and the mountain states. ~~I'm going to avoid~~ [He was going to avoid / He would avoid] cities and stop in small towns and ranches. Then ~~I'll go~~ [he would go] down the west coast from Washington and Oregon, and back through the southwest and south and up the east coast. Along the way ~~I'll just look~~ [he would just look / he was just going to look] and listen.

CHAPTER 9 REVIEW

Review Practice 9.1

Answers (Student's Book page 153)

1. The passage is formal writing. Why are there future forms other than *will*? *Some of the passage is quoted speech and uses future forms that are appropriate for that mode.*

2. Give an explanation for each of the future verb forms in the passage. Are they predictions, indefinite plans, definite plans, or scheduled events? *Formal writing uses* will: will sense, will call, will detect, will call; *Predictions*: is going to be, will look like, will reach; *Definite plans*: are introducing, are taking; *Scheduled event*: comes out

Review Practice 9.2

Answers (Student's Book page 154)

My company believes that our new product line ~~appeal~~ [will appeal / is going to appeal] to the American market, so we ~~exhibit~~ [are exhibiting / are going to exhibit] at a trade show in the United States next year. In fact, we've just signed a contract with an American consulting company. The consultants ~~make~~ [will make] all the arrangements for the trade show, and ~~I'm being~~ ['ll be OR will be] the contact person here in Japan. This is a big responsibility because the show is going to be our first venture outside of Japan. Next week, ~~I'm go~~ [go / 'm going] to Seattle for my first meeting with the consultants. I ~~leaving~~ [leave / 'm leaving OR returning] on Sunday and return on Saturday. Right now I'm working overtime because I'm getting ready for the trip. I ~~not~~ [won't] have time to see you while ~~I'm going to be~~ ['m] in the U.S., but I'll call you when I ~~will get home~~ [get home] again. The last time we talked, you and Katy ~~are going to start~~ [were going to start] looking for a house outside the city. How is that going?

Review Practice 9.3

Answers (Student's Book page 154)

To All Personnel:

Summer hours ~~are going to begin~~ [begin / will begin] on Tuesday, June 1, and end on Tuesday, September 7. During this time, the office ~~is going to close~~ [will close] at 1:00 every Friday. In order to make this early closing possible, the workday ~~is going to begin~~ [will begin] at 8:30 A.M. and end at 5:00 P.M. In addition, all personnel ~~are going take~~ [will take] 45 minutes for lunch instead of an hour. There ~~is going to be~~ [will be] no lunch break on Fridays.

Review Practice 9.4

Answers (Student's Book page 155)

Randy and I ~~will go~~ *are going* to Washington tomorrow. Our plane ~~will leave~~ *leaves* at 9:00 A.M. and ~~will arrive~~ *arrives* at 3:20 P.M. We'll stay at a hotel near the Capitol. *OR We're staying* The next morning, we'll take *OR we're taking* a tour to Mount Vernon, the home of George Washington. The tour ~~will leave~~ *leaves* at 9:30 and ~~will return~~ *returns* at 4:45 in the afternoon. After we'll ~~get back~~ *get back* from Mount Vernon, we'll play it by ear until we'll ~~leave~~ *leave* on Saturday. Of course, we'll see the Capitol, the White House, and some of the museums. And we definitely won't miss the Vietnam and Lincoln Memorials. But we'll relax too. This trip will be like a second honeymoon for us. *OR is going to be*

Review Practice 9.5

Answers (Student's Book page 155)

Right now I'm working, but tomorrow is Saturday and ~~I'll go~~ *I'm going* to the country to see my friends Mike and Lynn. They have a house in Rockland County and I'm going to stay *OR I'm staying* with them while the landlord ~~will paint~~ *is painting OR paints* my apartment. I decided to take the bus instead of renting a car. My bus leaves at 8:00 A.M. tomorrow and arrives about 10:30. They ~~pick me up~~ *'re picking me up* at the bus station. They have a swimming pool! I'm going to swim every day and work in their garden. And we're going to eat well—we always do that. *OR we'll eat* It ~~isn't being~~ *won't be* exciting, but that's OK with me. I haven't been away from the city all summer and I'm really looking forward to taking it easy for a few days.

Last year when I'm ~~there~~ *was*, we're ~~going to go~~ *were going to go* to the little country fair near their house. It ~~is~~ *was* really going to be fun, but it ~~rains~~ *rained* and we didn't go. We thought ~~we'll~~ *we'd* walk around and look at the farm animals. After that, we were going to have lunch and go on some of the rides. Maybe we'll go this year.

SECTION 3 REVIEW

REFRESHING YOUR MEMORY

Answers (Student's Book page 156)

1. What is the verb tense in this sentence? Why is it used?   *The simple present. The sentence expresses a general truth, and general truths are expressed with the simple present.*

2. What is the verb tense in these two sentences? Why is it used?   *The present perfect. The sentences express actions that began and ended at unspecified times in the past. This is one of the time frames expressed by the present perfect.*

3. What is the verb tense in these five sentences? Why is it used? What two time markers determine the tense?   *The simple past. The sentences express actions that happened at specified times in the past. This is one of the time frames expressed by the simple past. The time markers for the past are* at one time *and* some years later.

4. What tense are the italicized verbs in these sentences? Why is it used?   *The form (not strictly speaking a tense) is future in the past. The -ing verb phrases in these sentences have the same form as the past progressive, but these verbs do not describe events that were ongoing in the past. The writer is looking back at events that would have been expressed with* be going to *or* will *at the time they happened. This time frame is expressed by future in the past.*

Section Review Practice 3.1

Answers (Student's Book page 157)

An Amazing Meeting

I ~~have met~~ [met] my first boyfriend when I was in high school. He was an easygoing and humorous person, so we ~~have~~ [had] a lot of fun whenever we were together. Later, when we were preparing to take the university entrance examinations, we ~~are working~~ [were working] too hard to get together. My boyfriend studied hard, but he ~~fails~~ [failed] the examination. Then he ~~continues~~ [continued] studying in order to repeat it. I ~~was never getting in touch~~ [never got in touch] with him while he ~~is studying~~ [was studying], and so we lost contact with each other. Sometimes I missed him, but I ~~wasn't knowing~~ [didn't know] how to get in touch with him again. I thought I ~~will never see~~ [would never see] him again.

Twenty-three years later, my husband and I ~~decide~~ [decided] to move to the U.S. for our children's education. Before I ~~move~~ [moved], one day I met with my friends. At that time, my close friend ~~has told~~ [told] me that my ex-boyfriend was in the U.S. She ~~has met~~ [met*] him at a medical convention there. He ~~was wanting~~ [wanted] to see me.

                                             was
        At first I ~~am~~ hesitant. Koreans do not usually accept that married women meet their

                                    thought
ex-boyfriends. However, I ~~have thought~~ that I should meet him. I thought that he would

have good advice for me, and I was right.

        I have had a lot of problems living in the U.S. and educating my children. My ex-
                                                                        have absolutely needed
boyfriend has been living in the U.S. for twenty years more than me. I ~~have absolutely~~
          recommended
~~needing~~ his advice. He ~~recommend~~ that I should learn English in order to adjust to
                                          am   **am learning**
American life. That is why I ~~was~~ in this college and in this class. Now I ~~learn~~ English

and getting along much better in this country. Meeting my ex-boyfriend again has been a
                                was
great help to me, although it ~~is~~ a great shock when it happened. I was afraid that I ~~am~~
was going to have
~~going to have~~ problems because of him. Instead, my life is better.

*This could also be *had met,* but *met* is correct. The past perfect is not taught in *Nitty Gritty Grammar.*

Section Review Practice 3.2

Answers (Student's Book page 158)

No Fake Earthquake for Me!
have visited
        I ~~visited~~ most of the major tourist spots in Southern California. When I first arrived,
    went   **visited**
I ~~have been~~ to all of the large theme parks with wild rides. I ~~am visiting~~ Disneyland
                                    went
my first month in Los Angeles. Later, I ~~was going~~ to Knott's Berry Farm and then to
                        have also seen   **went**
Magic Mountain. I ~~am also seeing~~ all the best-known museums in the area. I ~~have~~

~~gone~~ to the Los Angeles County Museum a few years ago to see the exhibition of

the Impressionists. Shortly after that, I visited the Getty Museum, the Norton Simon

Museum, and the Huntington Museum.
                                    have not seen
        There is only one major tourist spot I ~~have not been seeing~~ yet, and that is Universal
                was going   **has**
Studios. I ~~am going~~ there last weekend, but I changed my mind. This theme park ~~had~~ a

simulated earthquake ride that is supposed to be very exciting and realistic. But I ~~have~~
have already experienced   **do not need**
~~already been experiencing~~ a real California earthquake. I really ~~am not needing~~ to pay for
                                'll just stay
a phony earthquake ride. Maybe next weekend I ~~just stay~~ home.

Section Review Practice 3.3

Answers (Student's Book page 158)

Yuri Umansky

Yuri Umansky has lived in the United States ~~since~~ *for* five years. When he first arrived in this country, he ~~has lived~~ *lived* in Michigan for six months. Then he and his family ~~were moving~~ *moved* to Dallas, Texas, for four and a half years. His first job was in a restaurant. He worked as a waiter. Since then, he ~~has~~ *has had* several other jobs, but he has worked as a bookkeeper in a hotel ~~since~~ *for* the last two years. Yuri ~~studied~~ *has studied* English for the last seven years, and he ~~has~~ *is still studying* ~~still studied~~ it at a community college near his home. He plans to continue taking classes in English and accounting. He ~~meets~~ *met* Lucie three semesters ago in Accounting 1, and they ~~are dating~~ *have been dating* since then. In fact, Yuri and Lucie ~~think~~ *are thinking* about getting married next year. Yuri ~~is going to ask~~ *was going to ask* Lucie to marry him on her birthday last month, but they ~~are both taking~~ *were both taking* exams then. Now he ~~asks~~ *'s going to ask* her on his birthday next week.

Modals

EXPLORING THE TOPIC

The passage "Sizing Up the Situation" is from the preliminary report by the 9/11 Commission, as it is usually called (the official name is The National Commission on Terrorist Attacks upon the United States). In addition to extensive study and investigation of the attacks by the commission's members and staff, twelve public hearings were held in 2003 and 2004. The preliminary report was first issued in the form of staff statements read aloud at the beginning of each session. This passage is adapted from the staff statement read at the first hearing, held in New York City on March 31 and April 1, 2003.

Answer (Student's Book page 160)

Which version tells you more about the FDNY's response?   *Although the use of modals has not yet been taught in* Nitty Gritty Grammar, *it is expected that students already understand their meanings well enough to see that Version 1 conveys more information. It tells us more about the feelings and decisions of the FDNY commanders, and also the commission's opinion about the situation and those decisions.*

Grammar Point 1 | **Modals: Present and Future Time**

This grammar point presents affirmative and negative forms of *could, might,* and *should* in present and future time. The same forms apply for *may* and *must. Can* and *have to* are treated separately in Grammar Points 3 and 4.

EXPLORING THE GRAMMAR POINT

Additional examples (Student's Book page 161)
* Everyone **should be** prepared for an emergency.
* In an emergency, you **should not use elevators**.
* Electric power **could go out**.
* Lights and elevators **might not work**.

UNDERSTANDING THE GRAMMAR POINT

Practice 1.1

Answers (Student's Book page 161)
1. Emergencies should not catch people unprepared.
2. In an emergency, you should not panic.
3. You should already know what to do.
4. An office emergency plan might be a good idea.
5. It could not be hard to make a plan.

6. We might be able to do it in a few hours.
7. It could save lives.

Modals: Past Time

This grammar point presents affirmative and negative forms for *could, might,* and *should* in past time. The same forms apply for *may* and *must*. Past forms of *can* and *have to* are treated separately in Grammar Points 3 and 4.

EXPLORING THE GRAMMAR POINT

Additional examples (Student's Book page 162)

• My family **could have reacted** better during the electric power blackout a few years ago.
• We **should have gone** to the store immediately and bought water, food, and ice.
• With ice, we **might have saved** some of the food in the refrigerator.
• We **shouldn't have wasted** time expecting the lights to come back on right away.

UNDERSTANDING THE GRAMMAR POINT

Practice 2.1

Answers (Student's Book page 162)

1. First, firefighters should have reported to their commanders.
2. They could have had lighter equipment.
3. They should not have tried to carry firefighting equipment up the stairs.
4. They might have been able to get more people down the stairs.
5. They should not have lost touch with each other.
6. They might not have been able to see each other.
7. They could have missed the order to leave the towers.
8. They should have received specific training for such disasters.

Can

Students are sometimes confused by the use of *could* both as a modal on its own (to express possibility), and as the past of *can*. If you feel this is the case for your students, you may wish to teach meaning (Grammar Point 5 and *could* in Grammar Point 6) before Grammar Point 3.

UNDERSTANDING THE GRAMMAR POINT

Additional examples (Student's Book page 163)

• **Present / future:** We think we **can paint** the house ourselves.
    We **cannot remodel** the kitchen without outside help.

• **Past:** We **could not begin** painting last month. We were too busy.
    We **could only choose** the colors.

As the only phrasal modal in the chapter, *have to* differs substantially in form from the other modals discussed.

EXPLORING THE GRAMMAR POINT

Additional examples (Student's Book page 164)
- We **had to find** a contractor to remodel our kitchen.
- He **has to finish** another job before he can begin.
- We **have to finish** working on the house before August.
- We'**ll have to take** some time off from our jobs in July.

UNDERSTANDING THE GRAMMAR POINT

Practice 4.1

Answers (Student's Book page 164)

1. Someone in this family (have to / think) __has to think__ about safety.
2. We (can / not / assume) __cannot assume__ that nothing will ever happen.
3. When Mitch woke up, he (can / smell) __could smell__ smoke.
4. He (have to / grab) __had to grab__ his dog and his photographs and run out of the house.
5. After the fire, Mitch (can / not / live) __could not live__ in his house for three months.
6. He (not / have to / stay) __did not have to stay__ in a hotel. He stayed with his sister.
7. Usually, when escaping from a fire, people think they (have to / leave) __have to leave__ the door open for firefighters.
8. Close the door! This (can / slow down) __can slow down__ the fire and save lives.

EXPLORING THE GRAMMAR POINT

Additional examples (Student's Book page 165)
- Some people **can learn** languages easily.
- Most adults **cannot speak** a new language without an accent.
- At the beginning of the semester, we **could not read** Spanish at all.
- Most of us **could speak** it only a little.
- We **could have learned** more easily in a Spanish-speaking country.
- I **can't go** to Spain next semester.
- Maybe I **can go** next year.

UNDERSTANDING THE GRAMMAR POINT

Additional example (Student's Book page 165)
- I **could have gone** this semester, but I had to finish my science requirement.

Practice 5.1

Answers (Student's Book page 166)

1. I had a hard time in Marseilles because I (speak) __couldn't speak__ French.

2. Estie (speak) __could speak__ French, although her accent was terrible.

3. I (try) __could have tried__ harder to communicate, but I let Estie do it.

4. Without discipline, we (solve) __cannot solve__ our problems.

5. With total discipline, we (solve) __can solve__ some of our problems.

6. A child's skill in reading (affect) __can affect__ his or her success in school.

7. Very young children (read) __cannot read__, but they (enjoy) __can enjoy__ listening to a story.

8. What will I do if I (find) __can't find__ a job after college? I (work) __can* work__ for my father, but I don't want to.

9. The class (be) __could have been__ interesting, but I didn't do the reading.

10. Americans know little about geography. In a study last year, many people (name) __could not name__ the capital of Germany.

*Could is also correct here, but it would express possibility (Grammar Point 6), not ability.

Grammar Point 6 ▶ Could, May, and Might

Nitty Gritty Grammar treats *could, may,* and *might* as interchangeable to express possibility. Many native speakers agree with this practice, as do many pedagogical and reference grammar books.

UNDERSTANDING THE GRAMMAR POINT

Additional examples (present / future) (Student's Book page 166)
- The organization **could change** its foreign language requirement soon.
- They **might decide** to require two foreign languages.
- They **may require** one non-European language like Chinese or Arabic.

You may wish to provide examples of these modals in the past as well.
- They **could have made** this change before I was hired.
- They **may* not have hired** me in that case.
- I **couldn't have learned** Chinese or Arabic.

*Some native speakers would consider this sentence incorrect, and would use *might* instead of *may*. However, many (perhaps most) native speakers do not make this distinction.

Practice 6.1

Answers (Student's Book page 167)

1. Evelyn Hong, 38, lives on Long Island. She recently resigned from the NYPD. She <u>could have accepted <i>or</i> may have accepted <i>or</i> might have accepted</u> a job with a police department on Long Island. They <u>could / may / might have offered</u> her more money. Or she <u>may / might not have felt like</u> driving two hours to work anymore.

2. William Johnson, 45, is thinking about his future. He <u>could / may / might retire</u> from the NYPD soon. He <u>could / may / might decide</u> to accept another police job in a smaller city. He <u>could / may / might make</u> less money there, but with his half salary from the NYPD, it would be enough.

3. Brad Sturgis, 28, shot a man while on duty, but did not kill him. The man was holding a very realistic-looking toy gun. Officer Sturgis <u>could / may / might not have realized</u> it was a toy. The man <u>could / may / might have refused</u> to put the gun down. The man was agitated. He <u>may / might not have known</u> that Sturgis was a police officer.

4. Lucy Solano, 35, is thinking about a career change. She <u>could / may / might resign</u> from the NYPD and <u>could / may / might take</u> a job in the ski resort town of Stowe, Vermont. It <u>could / may / might be</u> safer than New York City policing. Also, they <u>could / may / might offer</u> her the job of Police Chief.

5. Patrick Murphy retired last month. He <u>could not have been</u> 63 because he just turned 60 last year. He <u>could / may / might have decided</u> to spend more time with his grandchildren. Or he <u>could / may / might have wanted</u> to get serious about his golf game.

Grammar Point 7 **Must**

This grammar point discusses the use of *must* to express logical conclusions. Grammar Point 8 discusses its use as a synonym for *have to*.

EXPLORING THE GRAMMAR POINT

Additional information about the examples (Student's Book page 168)

The person whose finger is cut has not said that it hurts, and Chris has not said that he doesn't want to go to school. If they had said so, the situations would be certainties, not conclusions, and *must* would not be appropriate.

Additional examples
- The plumber **must be** here. His truck is in the driveway.
- Lisa never wants to pat Fluffy. She **must not like** cats.

UNDERSTANDING THE GRAMMAR POINT

Additional examples of *must* in the past

- Alana is really smart, but she only got a C on her history exam. She **must not have done** the reading.
- Joe's grades and SAT scores aren't wonderful, but he was accepted by an excellent college. He **must have had** a really good interview.

Practice 7.1

Answers (Student's Book pages 168–169)

1. Noriko is Japanese, but her last name is Martinez. Her husband __must be Hispanic__ .
2. Noriko has lived in Canada for ten years. She __must be familiar__ with Canadian culture by now.
3. I saw Noriko talking with Antonio. Antonio just arrived from Colombia recently and he speaks very little English. Noriko ____must speak____ Spanish.
4. Antonio showed Noriko some photographs of his children, but Noriko didn't show any photos to Antonio. She __must not have__ any children.
5. Noriko has several travel brochures for South America. She __must be planning__ a vacation.
6. Sometimes Noriko falls asleep in class. She __must not be getting__ enough sleep.

Practice 7.2

Answers (Student's Book page 169)

1. People must have written letters.
2. People must not have made many long-distance calls.
3. Everyone must have watched the same programs.
4. It must have been hard to stay in touch.
5. That must have been annoying.
6. People must not have watched movies at home.
7. People must have eaten at home more.
8. A lot of people must not have gone to college.

Grammar Point 8 ▶ *Must* and *Have To*

EXPLORING THE GRAMMAR POINT

Additional examples (Student's Book page 170)

- They **have to study** this weekend. The exam is on Monday.
- You **must not be** late for class. The teacher will not let you in.
- You **must have** permission to take this class.
- He **doesn't have to take** calculus. He took it in high school.
- Classes start Tuesday. We **had to register** last week.

UNDERSTANDING THE GRAMMAR POINT

Practice 8.1

Answers (Student's Book page 171)

1. To get a learner's license, applicants (take) __must take or have to take__ a written test, a vision test, and a hearing test.

2. To drive with a learner's license, there (be) __must be / has to be__ a licensed adult with you.

3. While you have a learner's license, you (receive) __must not receive__ a traffic conviction.

4. If you receive a traffic conviction, you (wait) __must wait / have to wait__ another year to get your license.

5. We (forget) __must not forget__ that traffic accidents are the number one killer of teens.

6. My friends and I got our licenses at sixteen. First, we (have) __had to have__ a learner's license for a year.

7. My friend Bud (get) __had to get__ glasses to pass the eye test, but I (get) __didn't have to get__ them. I already had glasses.

8. I (take) __had to take__ the road test three times because I couldn't parallel park.

9. Even after we got our regular licenses, we (have) __had to have__ an adult with us to drive late at night.

10. When you are eighteen, you can drive alone anytime. You (have) __don't have to have__ an adult in the car anymore.

Grammar Point 9 | *Might, Could, and Should*

This grammar point presents new present / future meanings of *might* and *could* and introduces *should*. (Grammar Point 10 addresses the past, where the meanings are different.)

EXPLORING THE GRAMMAR POINT

Additional examples (Student's Book pages 171–172)
- You **should begin** to save for your children's education as soon as they are born.
- You **should not wait** until they are in high school to start saving for college.
- You **might open** a special account at your bank.
- You **could put** money in it every month or from every paycheck.

UNDERSTANDING THE GRAMMAR POINT

Practice 9.1

Students are required to make judgments about the relative importance of the affirmative statements and express them with an appropriate modal. Students may have varying ideas of what is important, so some answers will vary.

Suggested answers (Student's Book page 172)

1. For safety, you (stay) __should not stay__ in a room with windows.

2. You (stay) __should stay__ on the first floor of your house. It is safer.

3. The electricity will probably fail, so you (want to rent) **might not want to rent** movies to watch during the storm.

4. You (reinforce) **should reinforce** the outside doors with plywood.

5. You (cook or heat) **should not cook or heat** with gas. You (turn off) **should turn off** the gas lines.

6. You (buy) **might buy / could buy** some cookies or other snacks to munch on during this stressful time.

7. You (listen) **should listen** to the radio or TV for official bulletins.

8. If there is an evacuation order, you (leave) **should leave** immediately.

9. If you leave, you (leave) **should not leave** your pets. You (take) **should take** them with you.

10. You (take) **might take / could take** some of your pets' toys with you, too.

| Grammar Point 10 | *Might Have*, *Could Have*, and *Should Have* |

Note that the meanings of the three modals in the past are different from their meanings in the present and future (covered in Grammar Point 9).

EXPLORING THE GRAMMAR POINT

Additional examples (Student's Book page 173)

- I got a "low pass" on the qualifying exam. I **could have studied** harder.
- I **might have joined** a study group. There was one on Tuesday nights.
- I **should have taken** this exam more seriously.
- I **should not have spent** so much time at the beach.

UNDERSTANDING THE GRAMMAR POINT

Practice 10.1

Students' choice of modals will vary. Answers will also vary in other ways.

Suggested answers (Student's Book page 174)

1. People could have decided where to go in advance, but they didn't. They wasted time thinking about this when the storm came.
2. People might have planned a safe escape route. More people could have reached their destinations safely.
3. People shouldn't have stayed in their mobile homes. Many of them were destroyed.
4. People could have left the coast. Some stayed and drowned in the storm surge.
5. People should have gotten away from the rivers quickly. Some were caught in the flooding.
6. People might have left sooner. The roads would have been open.
7. People should have left while it was still light. They could have escaped more easily.
8. People shouldn't have driven into moving water. Some cars were carried away.

CHAPTER 10 REVIEW

Review Practice 10.1

Answers (Student's Book page 176)

The San Francisco Earthquake of 1989

There was a major earthquake in San Francisco in 1989. It ~~must has been~~ **must have been** a

frightening experience for the residents. My grandparents were there, and they ~~could~~ **could have died**
~~have die~~ when their house collapsed, but they escaped. My grandmother's wedding ring

disappeared while she was escaping. It ~~might of come off~~ **might have come off** as she struggled to open the

door. Their neighbor also escaped from his house, then collapsed on the sidewalk. He

may have had a heart attack.

The quake occurred at rush hour, and many more people ~~should of be~~ **should have been** on the Nimitz

Freeway when part of it fell, crushing cars underneath. However, many people left work

early that day, so it may have been much worse. They ~~must go~~ **must have gone** home early to watch the

World Series on TV. Two local teams were playing, and that coincidence ~~may saved~~ **may have saved** some

lives.

The passage uses modals to express:

a. ability

(b.) possibility and logical conclusions

c. requirements and recommendations

d. mistakes

Review Practice 10.2

Answers (Student's Book page 177)

The April 15th Blues

We all ~~having to pay~~ **have to pay** our income taxes by April 15th. The envelope ~~must to be~~ **must be** at the

post office before midnight, and I always get there about 11:00 P.M. One problem is that

I'm very disorganized. My wife says I should ~~kept~~ **keep** my records in better order, but I never

do. Also, I just don't know enough about taxes. Probably I ~~should~~ **should hire** an accountant to do

them for me. Small business owners like me ~~not have to~~ **do not have to** hire an accountant, but some

people say I ~~must have hire~~ **must hire** one if I want to save money.

The passage uses modals to express:

a. ability

b. possibility and logical conclusions

(c.) requirements and recommendations

d. mistakes

Review Practice 10.3

Answers (Student's Book page 177)

First Fight

Last year was the first year we were married, and we prepared our tax return together.

Big mistake! We ~~should of see~~ *should have seen* an accountant. For one thing, our records were incomplete

and we ~~shouldn't guessed~~ *shouldn't have guessed* about some of our expenses. We ~~could have use~~ *could have used* some

professional advice about what to put down. But the main problem was that we made

each other crazy. We had our first big fight doing our taxes. Of course, we ~~should not~~ *should not have fought*

~~fought~~ about taxes, but with an accountant, we ~~might avoid~~ *might have avoided* the fight. We certainly ~~could~~

~~get over~~ *could have gotten over* it faster.

The passage uses modals to express:

a. ability

b. possibility and logical conclusions

c. requirements and recommendations

(d.) mistakes

Practice 10.4

Answers (Student's Book page 178)

Earthquake Country

Scientists believe that California ~~could has~~ *could have* a major earthquake at any time in the

next thirty years. It ~~should be not~~ *should not be* hard to imagine what might happen. The next major

earthquake ~~could damaging~~ *could damage* or ~~destroying~~ *destroy* older buildings. There ~~might could be~~ *might be / could be* fires.

Electrical service may be lost. Freeways ~~might been blocked~~ *might be blocked* and bridges ~~could fallen~~ *could fall*. All

of this is common knowledge. People who live in earthquake country ~~must to know~~ *must know* the

dangers. Nevertheless, people continue to move to high-risk areas. It just goes to show

that people ~~could ignore~~ *can ignore* almost anything.

The passage uses modals to express:

a. ability   c. requirements and recommendations

(b.) possibility and logical conclusions   d. mistakes

(Answer (a) may also explain the meaning of the last sentence.)

Review Practice 10.5

Answers (Student's Book pages 178–179)

1. Based on her driving, she should not have passed the road test.
2. We can't thank you enough.
3. The twins could read when they were four.
4. We should hurry.
5. We should have hurried.
6. We could / may / might be late.
7. We could / may / might be late.
8. They may not / might not have lived in Prague.
9. They could not have lived in Prague.
10. This should not take long.
11. I'm tired. You must be tired too.
12. She left on time. She should have been here an hour ago.
13. You must not smoke here.
14. He has to pay his taxes.
15. She had to pay her taxes.
16. You could / might save this money.
17. You should save this money.
18. You shouldn't spend this money.
19. I should have called you on your birthday.
20. I shouldn't have spent all the money.

Review Practice 10.6

Answers will vary.

Suggested answers (Student's Book page 180)

1. They must have lost their ball. It may have rolled into the street. It could be across the street or in the middle of the traffic. Their mother shouldn't have let them play near a busy street. They must be careful. They shouldn't try to get the ball by themselves. They should ask an adult for help. They might get their ball back.

2. They could be a father and daughter. The father could be in town on a business trip. They might be looking at photos of the daughter's vacation. She may have gone to Europe, maybe Greece. The family could be Greek-American, and she might have visited the town they came from originally. It is early in the evening and they don't have to leave the restaurant soon. They might stay until it closes. They must have a good relationship. They should get together more often.

3. They are a man and a woman. The woman must be in love with the man, but he must not be in love with her anymore. She may have thought they would get married, but now she must realize that he doesn't want to marry her. She shouldn't have trusted him. The man might be checking the time because he is late for work, or he might just want to get away from the situation. He may be trying to help, but he can't. He can only make things worse.

4. The young man may have been speeding. The police car could have been parked out of sight, and the young man must not have realized the officer was there. The cop may be annoyed because he is bored with waiting for speeders. He could also be a little envious of the younger man's motorcycle and the free time to ride it. The cop doesn't have to give the young man a speeding ticket—he can let him go with a warning. The young man should be very polite now. It could save him a ticket.

Conditionals

The conditional form discussed in Part 2 of this chapter is sometimes called the *present unreal*, or *second, conditional*. The two forms discussed in Part 3 are sometimes referred to as the *present real*, or *zero, conditional* and the *future real*, or *first, conditional. Nitty Gritty Grammar* does not discuss the *past unreal*, or *third*, conditional, which is also commonly taught in grammar classes, nor does it discuss the many other conditional forms used in speaking and writing. As you know, this book focuses on "the nitty gritty," the basics your students need first.

REFRESHING YOUR MEMORY

Answers (Student's Book page 181)

1. What is an independent clause?   *It's a clause that can stand alone as a sentence.*

2. What is a dependent clause?   *It's a clause that cannot stand alone as a sentence. It needs to be attached to an independent clause.*

3. Which kind of clause begins with a subordinator?   *A dependent clause*

4. What does a subordinator do in a sentence?   *It begins a dependent clause and connects it to an independent clause. It shows the relationship between the two clauses.*

5. What do the modals *can, may, might, could,* and *should* express in present and future time?   Can: *ability;* may: *possibility;* might: *possibility or suggestion;* could: *possibility or suggestion;* should: *advice*

EXPLORING THE TOPIC

The passage "Multi-Million-Dollar Granny" is from *The Rainmaker* by John Grisham. Grisham is an American lawyer and writer who specializes in "legal thrillers"—crime fiction about lawyers and the law. He writes approximately one novel a year, all of which have become best sellers. Many of his books have been made into movies, including *The Firm, The Pelican Brief, The Client,* and *The Rainmaker.*

Answers (Student's Book page 182)

1. ___If I had___ a grandmother worth twenty million dollars, ___I would send___ her flowers, cards, chocolates, and champagne.

2. ___If I had___ a grandmother worth twenty million dollars, ___I would call___ her once in the morning and twice before bedtime.

3. ___If I had___ a grandmother worth twenty million dollars, ___I would take___ her to church on Sunday.

4. __If I had__ a grandmother worth twenty million dollars, __we would go__ to brunch after church.

5. __If I had__ a grandmother worth twenty million dollars, __I would take care__ of her.

Grammar Point 1 ▸ Two Clauses

EXPLORING THE GRAMMAR POINT

Answers (Student's Book page 182)

What kind of clause are the ones in boldface type: independent or dependent?   *Dependent*

What kind are the other clauses?   *Independent*

What kind of word is *if*?   *A subordinator*

Additional examples
- **If you treat people well**, they appreciate it.
- He'll adopt a puppy next summer **if he moves to a bigger apartment**.
- **If I knew the answer**, I would tell you.

Grammar Point 2 ▸ Condition and Result

This grammar point discusses the functions of the two clauses in conditional sentences. It refers to the examples from Grammar Point 1.

UNDERSTANDING THE GRAMMAR POINT

Practice 2.1

Answers (Student's Book page 184)

1. __If I call Evangelina,__ we talk for at least an hour.
2. __Eileen might study finance__ if she went back to school.
3. __If Joe fixes his car,__ he can drive us to the conference next week.
4. If I could do anything I wanted __, I'd work for myself.__
5. You might make a lot of money __if you buy this stock.__
6. __If I had a million dollars,__ I'd buy a big house by the ocean.
7. __If the stock market crashes,__ I won't care because I don't own any stock.
8. If I go to the office on the weekend __, I usually come in late on Monday.__

Grammar Point 3 ▸ Meaning

EXPLORING THE GRAMMAR POINT

To teach the grammar point with books closed, you might use statements about your students. Make sure that the conditions (the *if* clauses) are clearly imaginary, and that the statements are in the present time frame.

You could say, for example, "If Marcus had an identical twin, he could take his brother's exams." Write some of your conditional sentences on the board, underlining the verb phrases. Then ask questions to demonstrate that neither the condition nor the results are real; they are imaginary: "Does Marcus have an identical twin? Does he take his brother's exams?"

UNDERSTANDING THE GRAMMAR POINT

To continue teaching with books closed, explain as in the Student's Book. For example, Marcus does not have a twin, and he is not going to take anyone else's exams. The condition (an identical twin) is imaginary, and so is the result (taking his exams).

| Grammar Point 4 | **Form: Present and Future** |

This conditional is sometimes called the *present unreal, present imaginary,* or *second* conditional.

EXPLORING THE GRAMMAR POINT

The grammar point focuses on the verb forms for unreal conditionals in the present and future. It is sometimes difficult for learners to understand (and accept) that past tense forms convey present and future meanings in such sentences.

Answers (Student's Book page 185)

What is the verb tense in the *if* clauses? *The simple past tense*

Describe the verb phrases in the main clauses. *They use modals.*

What do you notice about the verb *be* in sentence 1? *It is* were, *not* was, *even though* my brother *is singular.*

Additional examples
- If this **were** Friday, I **would go** to the movie at the Film Academy.
- If I **didn't have** an exam tomorrow, I **would go out** tonight.
- I **could call** Steve and tell him about Lara's accident if I **knew** his number.

UNDERSTANDING THE GRAMMAR POINT
Practice 4.1

Students must write reality-based conditional sentences about the tic-tac-toe game. The unreal condition for all of them is that the student is not player X or player O. Answers will vary.

Suggested answers (Student's Book page 186)
1. If I were X, I'd put it in square 8.
2. If I were O, I'd put it in square 7.
3. If I were X, I'd put it in square 3.

Practice 4.2

Some answers will vary.

Suggested answers (Student's Book pages 186–187)

1. If I were good with money, I might be rich someday.
2. If my brother were a stockbroker, I could do business with him.
3. If I didn't have a lot of credit card debt, I wouldn't worry about money all the time.
4. If I had a lot of money, I could invest in stocks.
5. If people were smart, they wouldn't overspend on their credit cards.
6. If I didn't pay my credit card bills on time, my interest rate would go up.

Grammar Point 5 ▶ General Truths and Habitual Actions

This grammar point describes the conditional that is the simplest grammatically. It is sometimes called the *present real, present factual,* or *zero* conditional.

EXPLORING THE GRAMMAR POINT

Additional examples (Student's Book page 187)

- If I **need** extra help, I **go** to the Writing Center.
- If there **is** a holiday, the library **is** closed.
- Students **have to make** an appointment if they **want** to see a counselor.

UNDERSTANDING THE GRAMMAR POINT

It may be interesting for your students to know that in conditional sentences about general truths or habitual actions, *if* can be replaced with *when.*

Practice 5.1

Answers will vary.

Suggested answers (Student's Book page 188)

1. If you already have a job, ___it is easier to find a new one.___
2. ___If you want a job___, you have to sell yourself.
3. If the interviewer likes a candidate, ___he or she gets a second interview.___
4. ___If jobs are hard to find___, employers can be very selective.
5. If someone has a poor reputation in the field, ___people do not want to hire him or her.___
6. ___If an interviewer asks a very personal question___, a candidate does not have to answer it.

Practice 5.2

Answers will vary.

Suggested answers (Student's Book page 188)

1. If I have a problem with my car, I take it to a mechanic.
2. If I need cash, I go to an ATM.
3. If I'm sick, I stay home from work.
4. If the plumbing breaks in my house, I turn off the water in the basement and call a plumber.

5. If I have trouble spelling a word, I use the spell-check feature on my computer.
6. If I feel sad, I call a friend and talk about it.
7. If I get hungry in the middle of the night, I just try to go back to sleep.
8. If I forget an appointment, I call and apologize and try to reschedule it.

Grammar Point 6 ▶ Conditional Predictions

This conditional is sometimes called the *future real, future factual,* or *first* conditional.

EXPLORING THE GRAMMAR POINT

This conditional form is sometimes taught with only *will* as the modal in the main clause. However, other modals are commonly used, and students have learned some of them in *Chapter 10, Modals.*

Additional examples (Student's Book page 189)
• If they **build** a new gym, better athletes **will apply** to the college.
• If I **save** some money, **I'm going to have** a big party for my birthday.
• If I **don't get home** too late, I **have to make** lasagna for dinner. I promised.

UNDERSTANDING THE GRAMMAR POINT

If you feel your students need more preparation before doing Practices 6.1 and 6.2, they could work in pairs to write sentences with each modal in the chart. As they are writing, check their work and send students to the board to write good examples. Then go over them with the class.

Practice 6.1
Answers will vary.

Suggested answers (Student's Book page 190)
1. If I drive faster, we might have an accident.
2. If you stay up, you'll be tired for school tomorrow.
3. If you play in the street, a car might hit you.
4. If you have ice cream now, you won't want to eat your dinner.
5. If you don't wear it, you might catch a cold.
6. If you don't wash them right now, you'll find out why!

Practice 6.2
Answers will vary.

Suggested answers (Student's Book page 191)
1. If you park here on Monday between 10:00 and 12:00, you could get a ticket.
2. If you drive down this street, you might have an accident.
3. If you don't wear a hard hat, you could be injured.
4. If you smoke here, they will ask you to stop.
5. If you try to use dimes and nickels, you won't get a soda.
6. If you walk on the grass, you could damage it.

Review Practice 11.1

Answers (Student's Book page 193)

1. What is the mistake in the sentence below?
   If I had time I would take a vacation.
   The sentence needs a comma after time.

2. Combine the following two clauses into one conditional sentence using *if*. In one clause, change *water* to a pronoun.   *If water reaches 100° Celsius, it boils. / Water boils if it reaches 100° Celsius.*

3. Read the following two sentences. In which one does the writer think it is more likely that the reader will learn some Spanish?
   a. If you learn some Spanish, you'll have more fun in South America next summer.
   b. If you learned some Spanish, you would have more fun in South America next summer.
   Sentence (a) is a real conditional. The writer thinks the condition may be met, and if it is, the result is certain. Sentence (b) is an unreal conditional. The writer thinks that the condition is not likely to be met, so the result is also unlikely.

Review Practice 11.2

Answers (Student's Book page 193)

Managing Your Credit Cards

There are hundreds of credit cards. If you ~~needed~~ **need** a credit card, you should shop

around and compare them. Look for a card with no annual fee and a low interest rate.

If you ~~will go~~ **go** to the Internet, you will find Web sites that compare dozens of cards.

Always pay your credit card bill on time. If you ~~were~~ **are** late, the bank ~~may charged~~ **may charge** you

a late-payment fee. If you ~~late~~ **are late** more than once (or sometimes only once), your interest

rate ~~go~~ **will go** up. It could double, triple, or more. If you pay the full balance on your credit

card every month, you will never get in trouble. However, if you ~~paid~~ **pay** only the minimum

payment every month, you ~~will soon has~~ **will soon have** a big balance—and a problem. For example, if

you ~~carrying~~ **carry** a balance of $4,000 on your credit card, and if the interest rate is 25%,

and if you ~~paying~~ **pay** only the minimum every month, it ~~takes~~ **will take** you 27 years to pay off your

balance, and it will cost you $12,000. You do not want that to happen. If you cannot

pay the full balance, at least you ~~pay~~ **should pay** more than the minimum payment.

Unfortunately, many people use a credit card to buy things they really cannot afford. If you keep a record of your credit card spending, you ~~always knew~~ *will always know* where you stand. Have a budget, and when you reach your limit for the month, stop spending!

Review Practice 11.3

Answers (Student's Book page 194)

The Automatic Millionaire

If I ~~can live~~ *could live* my life over again, I ~~will do~~ *would do* some things differently. I ~~will not buy~~ *would not buy* coffee on the way to work every day. If I needed coffee at my desk, I would take it from home. I ~~will buy~~ *would buy* my muffins at the supermarket and read the newspaper online. If I ~~do~~ *did* this, I ~~can save~~ *could save* at least $4 a day. If I saved $4 every workday, all year, that would be almost $1,000 a year. If I ~~can quit~~ *could quit* smoking, I ~~can save~~ *could save* another $1,500 a year. If I got just 4.5% interest on these savings every year, after ten years I would have more than $35,000!

Just from not spending money on coffee and cigarettes!

I found this out by reading a book called *The Automatic Millionaire,* by David Bach. There are many more ideas for saving money easily in this book. If I ~~was~~ *were* 20, and if I ~~follow~~ *followed* the advice in this book, I might become a millionaire in time to retire. But I'm 60!

It's too late for me to get rich. However, I have sent the book to two young women I know. If they take it seriously, they *can* get rich, and I hope they will.

Hope and *Wish*

REFRESHING YOUR MEMORY

Answers (Student's Book page 195)

1. What is an independent clause? *A clause that can stand alone as a sentence*

2. What is a dependent clause? *A clause that cannot stand alone as a sentence—it needs to be attached to an independent clause*

EXPLORING THE TOPIC

When Zlata began her diary, Sarajevo was still at peace. At first, she wrote about school work and birthday parties. When Serbian troops invaded the city, she began to write about bombings and death. In 1993, Zlata's diary was bought by a French publishing company that helped Zlata and her parents escape to France.

Answers (Student's Book page 196)

Zlata's Diary

Saturday, May 2, 1992 — The shooting started around noon. . . . Almost every window on

our street was broken. . . . I saw the post office in flames. . . . This has been the worst,

most awful day in my eleven-year-old life. I hope it will be the only one.
          that

Sunday, August 15, 1993 — We received a letter from Maja, Bojana, and Nedo. Nedo is

getting married on August 26. Maja is going to be the bridesmaid. Oh, I wish I could be
    that

there!

Wednesday, September 29, 1993 — Sometimes I wish I had wings so I could fly away
    that

from this hell. And that's impossible, because humans are not birds. That's why I have

to try to get through all this. I hope that it will pass and I will not suffer the fate of Anne

Frank. I hope I will be a child again, living my childhood in peace.
   that

EXPLORING THE GRAMMAR POINT

Answers (Student's Book page 196)

What kind of clause are the clauses with *that*: independent or dependent?   *Dependent*

What kind of clause comes immediately before *that*?   *Independent*

Additional examples

• People in trouble always hope **(that) other countries will send help**.

• Often, the other countries wish **(that) the problem would just go away**.

Grammar Point 2   *That*

UNDERSTANDING THE GRAMMAR POINT

Refer again to "Zlata's Diary" (or to the additional examples for Grammar Point 1) for examples of noun clauses that can either use *that* or omit it.

Practice 2.1

Answers (Student's Book page 197)

1. I'm sorry you're sick. I hope <u>you feel better soon.</u>

2. I had a wonderful time in Cancun, but I wish <u>I had not spent so much money.</u>

3. I made this sweater for you. I hope <u>it fits.</u>

4. This week seems so long! I wish <u>it were Friday.</u>

5. Edie came up with a wonderful idea. I wish <u>I had thought of it.</u>

6. My son and his girlfriend want to get married, but they're only 18. We hope <u>they will wait.</u>

7. I'm sorry. I didn't mean it. I hope <u>you can forgive me.</u>

8. The baby is so cute! I wish <u>you could see her.</u>

9. You're so smart. I wish <u>I had your brains.</u>

10. I left the house in a hurry this morning. I hope <u>I turned off the stove.</u>

Grammar Point 3   **Verb Tenses After** *Hope*

EXPLORING THE GRAMMAR POINT

Additional examples (Student's Book page 198)

• I hope you**'re having** a good time on your vacation.

• I hope you**'ll get** a nice tan at the beach.

• I hope you **relax** all week.

• I hope you **weren't sleeping** when I called yesterday.

• I hope you **got** to dinner on time.

• I hope I **can go** with you next time.

UNDERSTANDING THE GRAMMAR POINT

To use the chart, you might have students work in pairs to write sentences with *hope* and each form of *study*. While students work, have some of them go to the board to write their sentences. Correct the sentences on the board with the whole class.

Practice 3.1

Answers will vary.

Suggested answers (Student's Book page 199)

1. He hopes he <u>won't cut himself.</u>
2. He hopes there <u>is enough coffee for one cup.</u>
3. He hopes the rooster <u>will win some money.</u>
4. He hopes someone <u>has written to him.</u>
5. He hopes Alvaro <u>will give him a good price for the clock.</u>
6. He hopes she <u>won't tell them anything.</u>

Grammar Point 4 | **Verb Tenses After *Wish*, Present/Future**

EXPLORING THE GRAMMAR POINT

Begin with the cartoon on page 200. You might read it aloud or have two students read the two characters' parts. Make sure they understand that the last line means "I wish I knew why I keep wishing."

Answers (Student's Book pages 199–200)

What tense of the verb appears in the noun clauses that follow the main clause?   *The simple past*

What time frame do the sentences refer to, past or present / future?   *Present*

How do you know?   *There is no brief answer to this question. See* Understanding the Grammar Point *in the Student's Book.*

UNDERSTANDING THE GRAMMAR POINT

Of course, other verb forms can be used after *wish* besides those in the chart. For example, the cartoon uses *have to* + base form. However, the simple past tense, and *would / could* + base form are the most common and generally useful forms.

Practice 4.1

Answers (Student's Book page 201)

1. I wish I (enjoy) <u>enjoyed</u> my job more.
2. I wish my boss (be) <u>weren't</u> so hard to satisfy.
3. I wish we (have) <u>had</u> more time off.
4. I wish I (quit) <u>could quit</u> tomorrow.
5. I wish they (promote) <u>would promote</u> me to manager.
6. I wish they (give) <u>would give</u> me a raise.

7. I wish I (call in sick) <u>could call in sick</u> tomorrow.

8. I wish we (have) <u>didn't have</u> so many meetings.

9. I wish it (be) <u>were</u> 5:00.

10. I wish there (be) <u>were</u> some windows in this office.

Grammar Point 5 > Verb Tenses After *Wish*, Past

UNDERSTANDING THE GRAMMAR POINT

The term *past perfect* is introduced in the Student's Book. Please note that the past perfect is not taught as a verb tense in *Nitty Gritty Grammar* (which teaches only the most essential grammar for beginning writers). The term is used here only as a name for *had* (*not*) + past participle.

Additional examples (Student's Book page 201)
- I wish I **had studied** harder in college.
- I wish I **hadn't partied** so much.
- I wish I **could have graduated** with honors.

Practice 5.1

Students' answers should be true statements. Answers will vary.

Suggested answers (Student's Book page 202)
1. No. I wish I had made half that much.
2. No. I wish I had begun saving then.
3. No. I wish I could have learned to play then.
4. Not really. I wish I had been more popular.
5. No. I wish I could have bought them myself.
6. No. I wish it had been even 3.5.
7. No. I wish she had called because I had trouble with the homework.
8. No. I wish someone had given me one.

Grammar Point 6 > Events in the Present/Future

EXPLORING THE GRAMMAR POINT

Additional examples (Student's Book page 202)
- I **wish** I didn't have to work.
- I **hope** I'll fall in love with a woman who has lots of money.

UNDERSTANDING THE GRAMMAR POINT

Practice 6.1

Answers (Student's Book page 203)

1. I ___hope___ the war ends soon.

2. I ___hope___ my relatives are OK.

3. I ___wish___ I could help them more.

4. I ___wish___ that the countries next to mine could solve the problem.

5: Sometimes I ___wish___ I had stayed there to work for peace.

6. I ___hope___ the United Nations can negotiate a lasting peace.

Practice 6.2

Answers (Student's Book pages 203–204)

Anita and Barbara

My sisters Anita and Barbara differ a lot in their college plans and their career goals. Both of them are taking classes at Polk Community College. Anita (hope/wish) ___hopes___(1) she (finish) ___will finish___(2) in a few semesters and (transfer) ___transfer___(3) to a four-year college as an accounting major. Barbara is not sure yet what she wants to do. She (hope/wish) ___wishes___(4) she (transfer) ___could transfer___(5) to a four-year school, but she keeps changing her major and can't decide on a goal.

When I ask Anita and Barbara how important a career is to them, they give me different answers. Anita (hope/wish) ___hopes___(6) that she (find) ___will find / can find___(7) a job in an accounting firm as soon as she graduates. She also (hope/wish) ___hopes___(8) that she (have) ___will have___(9) her own small accounting business in two or three years. She has a lot of confidence in her plans for the future. But Barbara worries about making the wrong decision. She (hope/wish) ___wishes___(10) she (know) ___knew___(11) what to do with her life. Some people think that Anita is too optimistic and Barbara is too pessimistic, but I think they are both realistic about the choices they need to make.

EXPLORING THE GRAMMAR POINT

Additional examples (Student's Book page 204)
- I **hope** something can be done about global warming.
- I **wish** people had taken better care of the environment.

UNDERSTANDING THE GRAMMAR POINT

Practice 7.1

Answers (Student's Book page 205)

Lost Love

Brad and I dated all through high school. He wanted to get married as soon

as we graduated, but I wanted to wait. Now I (I/marry) _wish I had married_

him. I (he/think) _hope he didn't think / doesn't think_ that I didn't

love him. I just felt too young. I wanted to live a little first. I (I/know)

wish I had known / could have known how things were going to work out. But

of course that wasn't possible. In all these years, I've never met anybody as sweet as

Brad. I (he/change) _hope he didn't change / hasn't changed_ because of me.

No, I'm sure he's still the same. I (I/leave) _wish I hadn't left_ him, and I (he/forget)

hope he didn't forget me after I left. I've never forgotten him.

Grammar Point 8 — **Different Points of View**

This grammar point highlights the subjective nature of some choices between *hope* and *wish*. Note that this applies only to situations in the present and future. In the past, where the outcome has already been determined (even if it is not yet known), there is no such choice.

UNDERSTANDING THE GRAMMAR POINT

Additional examples (Student's Book pages 205–206)

Situation: The writer has just won a full scholarship to college.
- I **hope** my brother won't be jealous. I think he'll be happy for me.
- I **wish** my brother wouldn't be jealous, but I'm afraid he will be.

Situation: The writer wants to go to the beach.
- I **hope** the sun will come out, so we can go to the beach.
- I **wish** the sun would come out, but the forecast is for more rain.

Practice 8.1

Answers (Student's Book page 206)

1. Parinaz wishes she could lose ten pounds.
2. Parinaz wishes her boyfriend would stop smoking.
3. She wishes she could stay in the U.S. for a few more years.
4. She wishes her younger brother would come to the U.S. too.
5. She wishes she could get a scholarship next semester.
6. She wishes she could make more friends who speak English.

Practice 8.2

Answers will vary. See Student's Book page 206 for examples.

CHAPTER 12 REVIEW

Review Practice 12.1

Answers (Student's Book page 208)

1. a. __I__ We hope can buy a house someday.
   b. __C__ We hope we can buy a house someday.
   c. __C__ We hope that we can buy a house someday.

2. a. __C__ I hope I can meet him.
   b. __I__ I hope I could meet him.
   c. __I__ I wish I can meet him.
   d. __C__ I wish I could meet him.
   e. __C__ I wish I could have met him.
   f. __I__ I wish I would have met him.
   g. __C__ I wish I had met him.

3. 1. __a__ I hope he will be there.
   2. __d__ I hope they had a good time.
   3. __c__ I wish I had stayed there.
   4. __b__ I wish she would call me.

   a. The writer thinks this might happen.
   b. The writer thinks this probably will not happen.
   c. The writer regrets not doing this.
   d. The writer is worried that maybe this did not happen.

Review Practice 12.2

Answers (Student's Book pages 208–209)

September 3rd — I've finally decided to buy a new sofa. I've always liked my old sofa, but I've kept it too long. It is dirty, torn, and faded. I ~~hope~~ *wish* I had replaced it a long time ago. I hope I ~~could~~ *can* find a new one quickly. The problem is that my living room is small and most sofas are big. I'm going shopping tomorrow. I hope I'll be lucky.

September 17th — I went to all the furniture stores in town, and I wish I ~~wouldn't have~~ *hadn't wasted* ~~wasted~~ my time. Everything was too big. Finally, I decided to search online, and I found a sofa! It isn't wonderful, but I ~~wish~~ *hope* I'll like it well enough. They are delivering the new sofa tomorrow, so I threw out the old one to make room for it. I really ~~wish~~ *hope* I ~~would like~~ *will like / like* the new one.

September 18th — When they delivered the new sofa, I saw immediately that it was too big. And it is much too soft. I ~~hope~~ *wish* I ~~didn't accept~~ *hadn't accepted* it. I e-mailed Customer Service and

I was lucky. They agreed to take it back. They said seven to ten business days. I hope

they ~~came~~ **come** sooner. And I hope I can find another sofa before they come.

September 30th — They came an hour ago to pick up the sofa. I ~~wish~~ **hope** they ~~couldn't~~

~~damage~~ **won't damage / don't damage** it on the way back to the warehouse. I wish I ~~got~~ **had gotten** some proof that it was in

perfect condition. I went online again and found a sofa that I like a lot, and it's very

small. I ~~wish~~ **hope** I can find a store nearby where I can see it and sit on it. I'm not going to

buy anything I can't see first.

October 5th — I saw the little sofa today and I like it a lot. I wish I ~~found~~ **had found** it at the

beginning of this search. But this is custom furniture—they have to make it especially

for me. It isn't expensive, but it's going to take fourteen weeks! The salesperson says

sometimes they are faster and she ~~wishes~~ **hopes** they ~~could~~ **can** do it in twelve weeks, but I'm not

going to count on that. Anyway, I ordered it today. I ~~wish~~ **hope** I chose the right material. I

think I like it, but I wish I had brought home samples of the material first. I was in a

hurry. I ~~wish~~ **hope** I didn't make a mistake.

Review Practice 12.3

Answers (Student's Book page 209)

Broadway Bound

My son's sixth-grade class ~~wishes~~ **hopes** that they can all go to see "The Lion King" on

Broadway next June. They have already begun to raise money for the tickets, which are

going to cost $100 each. I wish the theater ~~gives~~ **would give** them a lower price, but the show is

very popular. Some of the kids hope they ~~could have earned~~ **can earn** the money by selling candy.

Others, including my son, are just asking people to give a dollar. My son went to all the

apartments in our building yesterday evening. I hope nobody ~~had gotten~~ **got** angry. There

are 55 apartments and he made $47. I was impressed. I wish I ~~know~~ **knew** how to make $47

that easily! I ~~wish~~ **hope** this works out for the kids. They are really excited about it. I wish my

daughter's class ~~did~~ **had done** things like this when she was in elementary school.

Hope and Wish   **137**

SECTION 4 REVIEW

REFRESHING YOUR MEMORY

Answers (Student's Book page 210)

1. In these sentences, do the modals express (a) ability / inability, (b) possibility, (c) a logical conclusion, (d) a requirement, (e) a recommendation, or (f) a mistake?

   <u>b</u>   This could be our lucky day.

   <u>e</u>   If your son is lonely, you could get him a dog.

   <u>a</u>   I couldn't hear the announcement.

   <u>c</u>   These shoes are size eight. They should fit you better.

   <u>f</u>   I should have called you yesterday.

   <u>d</u>   I have to go to class now. .

   <u>c</u>   That must have been wonderful.

2. In this sentence, which is the independent or main clause, (a) or (b)?   *b*
   Which is the dependent clause?   *a*
   Which clause expresses the condition?   *a*
   Which expresses the result?   *b*

3. Which writer is more optimistic about getting married?   *Writer B*
   Which is more pessimistic?   *Writer A*

Section Review Practice 4.1

Answers (Student's Book pages 210–211)

Being a Woman in Korea

A long time ago, Korean women ~~have to use~~ [had to use] only their last name without their first or

middle name. At that time, women were only good for having babies. If a wife didn't bear

a son, her husband ~~can take~~ [could take] a second or third wife. If she ~~does not accept~~ [did not accept] this, her

husband could divorce her. These days, women's status is higher than in the past, but it

is not greatly different. I have felt this in my own marriage. My husband was the oldest

son in his family, so he ~~have to had~~ [had to have] a son to carry on the family line. When I got

married, I ~~must have~~ [had to have] a son. However, I wanted to be in business, and I started my own

business before having a son. It was very successful and I made a lot of money.

In the meantime, my husband's business was not doing well. My mother-in-law

insisted that if women are successful, their husbands ~~could not succeed~~ [cannot succeed]. She said my success was blocking his. My husband actually agreed with his mother, and I finally

had to give up

~~must gave up~~ my business. At the same time, I also agreed to have a son. I thought

would survive

that if I had a son, my marriage ~~will survive~~, and it has. But truly, men still dominate

women in Korea.

Section Review Practice 4.2

Answers (Student's Book page 211)

My Hopes for This Class

hope

I expect a lot from this class. I ~~wish~~ that I will learn how to write English sentences

will understand

that are clear and understandable. If I learn this, then my employer ~~understands~~ what I

write. He will not say, "Vijitha, I got your note and it wasn't clear. Please explain what

I will learn   **write**

you mean." Next, I hope ~~will learn~~ how to organize my thoughts and ~~writing~~ them in

good paragraphs. My job now is taking care of two children, but I cannot help them with

can learn   **may be able**

their writing homework for school. If I ~~can to learn~~ to write well, I ~~may able~~ to help them.

may be able

Even more, someday I ~~may able~~ to help my own children with their homework and their

writing. Also, writing well could make a big difference in the future, when I finish college

and work in an office. I also hope that I will learn how to correct my mistakes in writing.

might / could / may learn

Eventually, I ~~might could learn~~ to avoid these mistakes in the first place. I really hope I

can do

~~could do~~ all of this in this class.

Section Review Practice 4.3

Answers (Student's Book page 212)

A Choice to Make

I should have finished college before I started working. Looking back, I'm not sure why
I didn't. It ~~must have been~~ *may / might / could have been* because I was tired of school. It ~~must have been~~ *may / might / could have been* because I

wanted to start making money—and spending it. It ~~must have been~~ *may / might / could have been* because I got a good

job, although it didn't last. That first job was working for my boyfriend. When we broke

up, I lost the job. After that, I ~~can never find~~ *could never find* such a good job again. Now I'm a middle-

aged woman with a nine-year-old son. It ~~can be~~ *may / might / could be* late for me to start something new in

my life, especially compared to the young people around me, but I ~~wish~~ *hope* it is not too

late. I believe that even if it is late, you ~~would~~ *should / can* try. The problem now is to decide what I

~~would study~~ *should study*. I was studying accounting when I dropped out of college before. If I choose

accounting again, I can use some of the credits I earned years ago. But I don't want to

study accounting. I want to be an elementary school teacher. If I try to do that, it ~~takes~~ *will take*

much longer, and I can't even go to school full time. I ~~must to keep working~~ *have to keep working* to pay the

bills. So, accounting or education? I hope I ~~would make~~ *make / will make* the right choice.

Prepositions

EXPLORING THE TOPIC

The Sun Also Rises (1926) was Ernest Hemingway's first full-length novel. It is the story of several Americans living in Europe—their friendships, love affairs, and rivalries. Hemingway worked on and off as a newspaper reporter throughout much of his life, often reporting on war and foreign affairs. During World War I, he was an ambulance driver for the American Red Cross, and later fought with the Italian army. A man of many passions, he was married four times, and died by his own hand in 1961.

About the questions

It is assumed that students are able to recognize enough correct and incorrect uses of the prepositions to answer the first question. Just one correct or incorrect preposition is enough to make the identification.

Answers (Student's Book pages 213–214)

Which is the correct version of the passage?   *Version 1*

Is the other version difficult to understand?   *No, mistakes with prepositions do not usually prevent the understanding of extended discourse. However, readers may be distracted by the mistakes.*

ABOUT PREPOSITIONAL PHRASES

This section is a quick tutorial on objects of prepositions and prepositional phrases, two concepts that are referred to in explanations in this chapter.

Answers (to the underlining task on Student's Book page 214)

In Bayonne (Version 1)

In the morning it was bright, and they were sprinkling the streets of the town, and we all had breakfast *in* a café. Bayonne is a nice town. It is like a very clean Spanish town and it is *on* a big river. Already, so early *in* the morning, it was very hot *on* the bridge across the river. We walked out *on* the bridge and then took a walk through the town. . . .

We found out *at* the tourist office what we ought to pay for a motor-car to Pamplona and hired one *at* a big garage. . . . The car was to pick us up *at* the hotel *in* forty minutes, and we stopped *at* the café *on* the square where we had eaten breakfast. . . . It was hot, but the town had a cool, fresh, early-morning smell, and it was pleasant sitting *in* the café.

EXPLORING THE GRAMMAR POINT

Additional examples (Student's Book pages 214–215)

- Liliana lives **in** Canada. (country)
- She has a house **in** Nova Scotia, **in** the Maritime provinces. (province / region)
- She works **in** Montreal for two or three months a year. (city)
- She has a small apartment **on** St. James Street **in** Old Montreal. (street / neighborhood)
- Her Montreal office is **at** 696 St. Catherine Street. (address)

UNDERSTANDING THE GRAMMAR POINT

As a follow-up, you might elicit the names of countries, regions, states or provinces, cities, neighborhoods, and addresses that are known to your students. Have them say or write sentences beginning, "I live / study / work . . . ," or "I have lived / studied / worked . . . ," and using appropriate prepositions.

Practice 1.1

Answers (Student's Book page 215)

Washington or Washington?

When I first lived _____in_____ the U.S. as a child, I confused Washington, D.C.,

1

with the state of Washington. When I heard that the president lived _____in_____

2

Washington, I thought of Washington State. The fact is that the president lives in the

White House _____in_____ Washington, D.C. Once a person is _____in_____ the right

3   4

Washington—Washington, D.C.—the White House is not hard to find. It's _____on_____

5

Pennsylvania Avenue, not far from the Washington Monument, which is _____on_____

6

Fifteenth Street. The White House is _____at_____ 1600 Pennsylvania Avenue, N.W. Next

7

week I'm taking my kids on a trip to Washington and the South. We'll be _____in_____

8

Washington (D.C.!) for three days and _____in_____ the South for a week. _____In_____

9   10

Washington, we're staying with my sister _____in_____ the Adams-Morgan neighborhood.

11

EXPLORING THE GRAMMAR POINT

Additional examples (Student's Book page 216)

- I usually study **in** my bedroom.
- I'll meet you **in** the lobby.
- They have a cabin **in** the mountains.
- There's a mirror **on** the wall over there.
- No one was home, so I waited **on** the steps.
- There was no label **on** the bottle.
- Jill and Richard are **at** the movies.
- Ron is swimming **at** the gym.
- They're spending their vacation **at** the lake.

UNDERSTANDING THE GRAMMAR POINT

Practice 2.1

Answers (Student's Book page 216)

1. on   2. at   3. in ·

To follow up, use things in the classroom to elicit sentences with prepositions. For example, point to things that are **on** the desk / floor / wall; **in** the corner, the wastebasket, your bag, or pocket. Position yourself to prompt sentences with **at** the door / window / desk / front of the room / back of the room.

Practice 2.2

You might do this practice in class, first reading the speech bubbles aloud and saying "blank" where there are blanks to be filled in. Then give students a few minutes to read the comic strip silently and fill in the blanks. Finally, have students read the completed speech bubbles aloud. Write the correct preposition on the board as each speech bubble is read.

Answers (Student's Book page 217)

I'm down __at__ your corner.

I'm __at__ the market.

I'm __at__ Normy's house.

Momma, I'm __at__ the cleaner's.

I'm back __at__ your corner.

I'm __in__ the kitchen.

Practice 2.3

Answers (Student's Book page 218)

1. Before you start painting, you have to mix the paint __in__ the can.

2. Be careful where you put the lid of the can because there is paint __on__ it.

3. As you paint, you put paint __on__ your brush, and then __on__ the surface you are painting.

4. When you begin, all the paint is __in__ the can.

5. As you continue painting, you get paint __on__ the outside of the can too.

6. Soon you may have some paint __on__ your hands.

7. To avoid this, don't hold the paint can __in__ your hand.

8. Put it __on__ the floor, __on__ an old newspaper or a rag.

9. If you take a break, leave the paintbrush __in__ the can, not __on__ the can or __on__ the newspaper because the paint might begin to dry.

10. When you finish painting, if there is still paint __in__ the can, put a small amount of water __in__ the can too.

11. Put the lid __on__ the can very tightly.

12. Store the can __in__ a cool place.

Grammar Point 3 ▸ Events

EXPLORING THE GRAMMAR POINT

Additional examples (Student's Book page 218)

- No one is here. They're all **at the funeral**.
- Edith and Mark met **at her sister's wedding**. They've been married for five years now.
- The office is closed tomorrow. Everyone will be **at the conference**.

UNDERSTANDING THE GRAMMAR POINT

Practice 3.1

Students apply guidelines for *at* that were presented in Grammar Points 2 and 3.

Answers (Student's Book pages 218–219)

1. Enrique was tired when he arrived. He actually fell asleep at a family get-together [E]
   at his brother's house. [L]

2. There were a lot of relatives at the rehearsal dinner [E]. It was at a restaurant [L] in San Angel.

3. He met an old friend at the wedding reception [E], which was held at the same [L]
   place as the rehearsal dinner.

4. Yesterday he was at an art gallery [L], at an auction [E].

5. Next weekend he'll have fun at a dance [E] at the club [L].

6. Before he leaves, he'll see everyone one more time at a picnic [E]. They're going
   to have it on one of the boats at the "floating gardens" [L] of Xochimilco.

Practice 3.2

Answers (Student's Book page 219)

First Date

I met my wife _____on_____ the subway. We both got on the train _____at_____
1   2

Times Square. It was very crowded _____in_____ the car, and I apologized for bumping
                                         3

into her. We began talking, and then we both got off _____at_____ South Ferry. We stood
                                                           4

_____on_____ the platform _____in_____ the station for twenty minutes, just talking.
5   6

Then we both realized we had to be _____at_____ work. Carol gave me her phone
                                         7

number and I put it _____in_____ my pocket. As soon as I was _____at / in_____ the office,
                          8   9

I called her and we made a date for the next night. We arranged to go to the movies. We

were going to meet _____at_____ the Clearview Cinema _____on_____ 23rd Street. We
                         10   11

would meet _____on_____ the sidewalk if it was nice. If it was raining, we would meet
                  12

_____in_____ the lobby.
13

That night, I arrived _____in_____ a taxi and looked for Carol. She wasn't _____at_____
                            14   15

the theater, either outside or inside. I waited and waited. The show started, and still no

Carol. Finally I decided she must have changed her mind. As I was leaving, Carol ran up

to me, breathless. There are two Clearview Cinemas _____on_____ 23rd Street,
                                                          16

one _____at_____ Seventh Avenue and one _____at_____ Eighth! She had been
        17   18

_____at_____ the other theater. So I found my wife _____on_____ the subway, but I almost
19   20

lost her _____at_____ the movies.
              21

Optional activity

Have students brainstorm different kinds of events and list them on the board. Have students
write a sentence for each of five events, using a preposition + the name of the event. Some
students could work at the board.

Example

My grandparents danced all night **at their fiftieth wedding anniversary party**.

EXPLORING THE GRAMMAR POINT

Answers (to the underlining task on Student's Book page 220)

1. We were there in 1999.

2. We went in the summer, which was the rainy season.

3. It rained in the morning, afternoon, and evening almost every day.

4. In July, we stayed in an old colonial-style hotel.

5. They served tea at 4:00.

6. Sometimes there was dancing at night.

7. On July 15th, there was a small earthquake.

8. It happened on Thursday, when we were at the beach.

UNDERSTANDING THE GRAMMAR POINT

Optional activity

Play a game with two teams. Have students brainstorm time expressions (without prepositions) and write them on the board. (For control, you may want to prompt them: "Give me a year. Give me a month. . . .") Then point to items in the list (do this in random order) while individuals on the two teams take turns saying the correct prepositional phrase (*in / on / at* + the time expression). One point for each correct answer.

Grammar Point 5 *Every* and *All*

EXPLORING THE GRAMMAR POINT

Additional examples (Student's Book page 221)

- **Incorrect:** I go to the gym **in every afternoon**.
  Correct: I go to the gym **every afternoon**.

- **Incorrect:** I can never sleep **at all night**.
  Correct: I can never sleep **all night**.

- **Incorrect:** There's a parade **on every Fourth of July**.
  Correct: There's a parade **every Fourth of July**.

UNDERSTANDING THE GRAMMAR POINT

You could follow up by having students write sentences in pairs using *all / every* + a time expression. Have them read their sentences aloud.

UNDERSTANDING THE GRAMMAR POINT

Additional examples (Student's Book page 221)

Past Time

• **Last summer**, we spent a week at Lake Tahoe.

Future Time

• I'm leaving work early **this afternoon**.
• **Next August**, Kay is going to start walking across the United States.

Practice 6.1

Answers (Student's Book page 222)

Arriving in Ghana

The first foreign country I lived in was Ghana, West Africa. ___In___ 1966, I
took a three-month training program to be a teacher there. My group arrived in Ghana

___in___ January, 1967. ___In___ the dry season, the *harmattan* winds

blow red dust down from the Sahara. When we got off the plane ___at___ four

___in___ the afternoon, the sky was red and the sun was a dim red ball. Also, I

smelled smoke from cooking fires and other scents I didn't recognize. Suddenly I knew I

was a long way from home.

We got there ___on / —___ Saturday, and ___on / —___ Sunday, ___at___

sunrise, trucks began arriving to take us to our schools. The truck came from my school

___in___ the late afternoon. We arrived in the village ___at___ night, they took

me to my house, and I fell into bed and slept. ___In___ the morning, there was a

staff meeting at the school. ___On / —___ the following day, ___on / —___ January 16th

___at___ 7:00 A.M., I faced my first class as a teacher.

Practice 6.2

You might assign this open-ended exercise for homework or do it in class as pair work. To
correct it, you could have students write sentences on the board where you can go over them
with the whole class. While students are writing on the board, move around the class looking
at all the papers and give some feedback to each student.

CHAPTER 13 REVIEW

Review Practice 13.1

Answers (Student's Book page 223)

1. There is a poster of Venice __on__ the wall __in__ my room.
   Explanation: Use *on* for surfaces. Use *in* for enclosed areas.

2. I'll see you __—__ next weekend.
   Explanation: When *next* precedes a time expression, the phrase often does not take a preposition.

3. Rob isn't here. He's __at__ a ball game __in__ Springfield.
   Explanation: Use *at* for events. Use *in* for cities.

4. Edith is __at__ the store. She'll be back soon.
   Explanation: Use *at* for general locations.

5. I love watching the fireworks __on__ the Fourth of July.
   Explanation: Use *on* for holidays.

Review Practice 13.2

Answers (Student's Book page 224)

My Pain-in-the-neck Allergies

My allergies are a pain ~~at~~ *in* the neck. To start with, I have to get shots every week. I go to the doctor ~~in~~* every Tuesday afternoon, ~~on~~ *in* the middle of my busy day. The doctor's office is ~~at~~ *in* Long Beach, ~~at~~ *in* the busiest part of town. It is in a tall building ~~in~~ *on* Long Beach Boulevard with very little free parking nearby. I usually have to park ~~at~~ *in* a parking lot. After lunch, the office opens ~~in~~ *at* 2:00 P.M., and I usually have my appointment ~~in~~ *at* 2:30. After I stop at the receptionist's desk, I often have to wait for almost an hour ~~at~~ *in* the waiting room. It's usually very noisy ~~at~~* there, because everyone is talking ~~in~~ *on* their cell phones. I try to remember to bring my CD player, so I can put on my headphones and listen to music, instead of all the noisy patients. After all that aggravation, I get one shot ~~on~~ *in* each arm. To make things worse, I have to pay for the shots ~~in~~* every month, and they're expensive. Not only are allergies a pain ~~at~~ *in* the neck, they're also a pain in the wallet.

*No preposition.

Review Practice 13.3

Answers (Student's Book page 225)

Arrival

        There was no one ~~on~~ *in* the train station. On the other side of the street, ~~at~~ *on* the sidewalk shaded by almond trees, only the pool hall was open. The town was floating ~~at~~ *in* the heat. The woman and the girl got off the train and crossed the abandoned station—the tiles were split apart by the grass growing up between—over to the shady side of the street. It was almost two. ~~In~~ *At* that hour, weighted down by drowsiness, the town was taking a siesta. The stores, the town offices, and the public school closed ~~on~~ *at* eleven and didn't reopen until a little before four, when the train went back. Only the hotel across from the station, with its bar and pool hall, and the telegraph office ~~in~~ *on* one side of the plaza stayed open. The houses, most of them built on the banana company's model, had their doors locked from the inside and their blinds drawn. ~~On~~ *In* some of them it was so hot that the residents ate lunch ~~at~~ *on* the patio. Others leaned a chair against the wall, ~~on~~ *in* the shade of the almond trees, and took their siesta right out ~~at~~ *in* the street.

Review Practice 13.4

Answers (Student's Book page 226)

Leaving Fuling

I left Fuling ~~at~~ *on* the fast boat to Chongqing. It was a wet, rainy morning ~~on~~ *in* June—the mist was thick ~~in~~ *on* the Yangtze like dirty gray silk. ~~At~~ *In* the morning, I said goodbye to the other teachers, and then I headed down to the docks in a car from the college. The city rushed past, gray and familiar ~~on~~ *in* the rain.

A few of the students came to see me off, along with Dean Fu. I shook hands awkwardly and boarded the boat. Karaoke videos played ~~at~~ *on* the television screen while we sat there on the dock for thirty minutes. I watched the students standing ~~at~~ *in* the rain and wondered what their futures would be like. William was going off to teach ~~on~~ *at* a private school ~~at~~ *in* the eastern province of Zhejiang; Mo Money was looking for business jobs in Fuling; Luke would be married in October, ~~in~~ *on* National Day.

The boat pulled out of the harbor. The students stood perfectly still ~~at~~ *on* the dock. Behind them, the city rose, gray and dirty-looking ~~on~~ *in* the mist. It was hard to believe that for two years this place had been my home. I wondered when I would see it again, and how it would be changed.

Word Forms

REFRESHING YOUR MEMORY

Answers (Student's Book page 227)

1. _____**Verbs**_____ express actions, states, or situations.
2. _____**Nouns**_____ name people, places, things, concepts, or activities.

EXPLORING THE TOPIC

The passage "The Purple Invader" was written for *Nitty Gritty Grammar* in the style of a Web encyclopedia entry.

The task reinforces students' understanding of nouns and verbs and focuses their attention on adjectives and adverbs that modify them.

Answers (Student's Book pages 227–228)

The Purple Invader

(Purple) *loosestrife* is an (invasive) *plant* that *arrived* (accidentally) from Europe in the (early) *1800s*. It has (no natural) *enemies* in North America, so its distribution today is from Canada to Mexico. The *plant* is (beautiful,) with (showy) *spikes* of (purple-pink) *flowers* on (very tall) *stems*. Unfortunately, purple loosestrife provides neither food nor shelter for (native) *wildlife*. It grows in (wet, marshy) *areas*, where it *spreads* (rapidly) and (soon) *crowds out* (native) *plants*.

Grammar Point 1 ▶ **Adjectives and Adverbs**

EXPLORING THE GRAMMAR POINT

Answers (Student's Book page 228)

1. **Adjectives:** a. He wrote a **long** <u>report</u>.

               b. All of his <u>facts</u> were **correct**.

2. **Adverbs:**   a. He <u>writes</u> **fast**.

               b. He **always** <u>checks</u> his facts.

Additional examples

- **Adjectives:** A **small** <u>drill</u> is a **handy** <u>tool</u>.
- **Adverb:**   It <u>should be used</u> **carefully**, with safety glasses.

EXPLORING THE GRAMMAR POINT

Additional examples (Student's Book page 229)

• Let's **plant** a garden this year. (verb)

Last year every **plant** in my garden died. (noun)

• These are my **best** clothes. (adjective)

I did my **best**. (noun)

• She drives a really **fast** car. (adjective)

She drives **fast**. (adverb)

She's on a juice **fast** right now. (noun)

I'm going to **fast** for a day. (verb)

UNDERSTANDING THE GRAMMAR POINT

You might follow up by referring students again to "The Purple Invader" on page 228. Have them identify each italicized word as a noun or verb and say whether its modifier is an adjective or an adverb.

Grammar Point 3 ▸ **Identifying Parts of Speech by Word Endings**

EXPLORING THE GRAMMAR POINT

Additional examples (Student's Book page 229)

• His parents made sure he got a good **education**.

• Could you **summarize** this article for me, please?

• Her parents are both **successful** lawyers.

• That suit fits you **perfectly**.

UNDERSTANDING THE GRAMMAR POINT

Practice 3.1

The word endings in the passage include some that have not yet been presented. Students should be able to recognize them as word endings even though they have not studied them yet.

Answers (Student's Book page 230)

Public Speaking

Giving a *talk* (n.) in front of an audience can be *frightening* (adj.), but if you *plan* (v.) *ahead* (adv.), you will be *satisfied* (adj.) with the *results* (n.). Here are some tips to help you give a *successful* (adj.) talk.

1. Don't let the *walk* (n.) to the *front* (n.) of the room frighten you. *Walk* (v.) *slowly* (adv.) and *breathe* (v.) *deeply* (adv.). Turn *confidently* (adv.) toward your audience.

2. If you *panic* at first, take a *deep breath* and try *again.* The *panic* will go away.

   [v.] [adj.] [n.] [adv.] [n.]

3. If your talk is more than five minutes long, *request* a *glass* of *water.* Drinking some *water* will give you a *good* reason to *pause,* and *pauses* can help you maintain your *concentration.*

   [v.] [n.] [n.] [n.] [adj.] [v.] [n.] [n.]

4. *Trust* your audience. They want you to succeed, so give them your *trust* from the *start.*

   [v.] [n.] [n.]

5. Talk about something you are truly *interested* in. Your *interest* in your topic will *automatically* *interest* the audience in what you have to say.

   [adj.] [n.] [adv.] [v.]

6. Practice your talk in advance. Be *careful,* but don't worry too much about mistakes. Certainly don't *apologize!* Everyone makes mistakes.

   [adj.] [v.]

Grammar Point 4 **Changing Verbs to Nouns**

EXPLORING THE GRAMMAR POINT

Additional examples (Student's Book page 231)

• They **attend** class every day.
• The class does not **require** much work. The only **requirement** is perfect **attendance.**
• My daughter needs to have a **discussion** with her **counselor.**
• I want him to **counsel** her about college and **discuss** her options.

UNDERSTANDING THE GRAMMAR POINT

Completing the chart is both a comprehension check and a controlled practice of the new word endings. There are various ways to have students complete the charts in this chapter. Here are three different suggestions for use with any of the charts:

• Have students work in pairs or groups, sharing their knowledge of vocabulary.

• Have students work alone or in pairs, using a learner's dictionary.

• With books closed, write the words from the box on the board in alphabetical order. (In this first chart, the words are verbs.) Then say and write an ending (for example, *-ment*), and have students call out possible combinations of word + ending, guessing if they wish. (In this chart, the combinations are nouns.) Write correct combinations next to the corresponding words on the board as students say them:

assign	assignment
attend	attendance
counsel	counselor
differ	difference
discuss	discussion

motivate	motivation
require	requirement
reserve	reservation

Finally, have students complete the chart in their books with the original words and new combinations (here, verbs and nouns) from the board.

In this chart, there is only one correct noun for each verb in the word box. Some of the verb + word ending combinations require spelling changes, but spelling is not the focus of this grammar point. You might point out the spelling changes as you go over the answers, but for most classes it will be better not to give rules for them.

Answers (Student's Book page 232)

VERBS TO NOUNS		
Verb	**+ Ending**	**= Noun**
agree	**-ment**	agreement
assign		assignment
require		requirement
accept	**-ance/-ence**	acceptance
prefer		preference
attend		attendance
differ		difference
educate	**-tion/-sion/-ation**	education
comprehend		comprehension
inform		information
discuss		discussion
motivate		motivation
reserve		reservation
erase	**-er/-or**	eraser
educate		educator
counsel		counselor

Practice 4.1

Some of the nouns in this practice are in the chart on page 232 of the Student's Book, and some are not. If the task is challenging for your students, you might let them work in pairs or use a learner's dictionary for support.

My Former Instructor, Mrs. Albelo

Mrs. Albelo was one of the best (instruct) _____instructors_____ I have ever had.
₁

She won the (admire) _____admiration_____ of most of her students. For one thing,
₂

her style of classroom (manage) _____management_____ was effective. She required
₃

regular (attend) _____attendance_____. She stressed coming to class on time and
₄

handing in all (assign) _____assignments_____ on their due date. Also, she always
₅

announced (examine) _____examinations_____ a week ahead of time. Second, she was an
₆

expert in (motivate) _____motivation_____. For example, she always made (discuss)
₇

_____discussions_____ interesting, and the (inform) _____information_____ she
₈ ₉

presented often came within humorous stories. These stories encouraged us to use our

(imagine) _____imagination(s)_____, which added to our (enjoy) _____enjoyment_____
₁₀ ₁₁

of the class. Third, Mrs. Albelo made it clear that she cared for all her students.

She often stayed after class for (converse) _____conversation_____. This attitude
₁₂

made a big (differ) _____difference_____ to us. I'm really glad that my (counsel)
₁₃

_____counselor_____ recommended Mrs. Albelo to me. She made getting an (educate)
₁₄

_____education_____ a pleasure.
₁₅

Grammar Point 5 ▶ Changing Adjectives to Nouns

EXPLORING THE GRAMMAR POINT

Additional examples (Student's Book page 233)

- Some people are just not **able** to be **kind**.
- Her **ability** is **equal** to her **kindness**.
- Racial **equality** is part of his **idealism**.
- I have the **ideal** job.

UNDERSTANDING THE GRAMMAR POINT

There is only one correct noun for each adjective in the word box. See Grammar Point 4 in this Teacher's Manual (page 153) for suggestions on using the chart.

ADJECTIVES TO NOUNS		
Adjective	**+ Ending**	**= Noun**
kind	-ness	kindness
sleepy		sleepiness
playful		playfulness
ugly		ugliness
secure	-ity	security
real		reality
able		ability
equal		equality
parallel	-ism	parallelism
active		activism
elite		elitism
ideal		idealism

Practice 5.1

Some of the nouns needed for this exercise are in the chart on page 234 of the Student's Book, but most are not. If the task is challenging for your students, you might let them work in pairs or use a learner's dictionary for support.

Answers (Student's Book pages 234–235)

The Children in the Yard Next Door

The kids next door inspire me when I watch them playing in their yard. When they

shout and run out onto the grass in the morning, their (loud) _____loudness_____
                                                                        1

does not bother me. Instead, I appreciate their sounds of joy and (happy)

_____happiness_____ . They ignore the (ugly) _____ugliness_____ in the
          2   3

street and focus on the beauty and (pleasant) _____pleasantness_____ of their own
                                                          4

world. The children's attitude inspires me to think about how I can put more (playful)

_____playfulness_____ into my own life. Their (active) _____activity_____ inspires
          5   6

me to be more energetic. And their (curious) _____curiosity_____ makes me
                                                        7

want to find out more about the world around me. At the end of the day, I notice the children's (tired) _____**tiredness**_____ , and I recognize my own need for rest. I am

                                    8

also grateful because these wonderful children have helped me remember the (ideal)

_____**idealism**_____ that I almost left behind in childhood.

              9

Changing Nouns to Adjectives

EXPLORING THE GRAMMAR POINT

Additional examples (Student's Book page 235)

• Do you have a **moment**?

  Don't worry. It's nothing **momentous**.

  There was a **momentary** power failure during lunch.

• I learned the **elements** of baseball when I was in **elementary** school.

  When I smelled smoke, I felt an **elemental** fear.

• The dentist hit a **nerve**.

  Going to the dentist makes me **nervous**.

  She'll try anything. She's really **nervy**.

UNDERSTANDING THE GRAMMAR POINT

This chart is challenging because there are eight different endings. Moreover, some nouns in the box can form more than one adjective with the endings in the chart. The following procedure can limit the challenge of the task and reduce the time needed for it:

1. Have students work in seven pairs or groups. Assign each group one word ending from the chart, omitting -*less*. Have students share their knowledge or use learner's dictionaries to make all the adjectives they can with the fifteen nouns in the word box + their group's ending.

2. Now do -*less* with the same seven groups. Assign the fifteen nouns in the word box (omitting *luck*, the example) so that each group has two or three nouns, including at least one that forms an adjective with -*less*. For example:

1	2	3	4	5	6	7
moment base(less)	nerve(less) boy	success power(less)	count(less) noise(less)	sleep(less) fool	limit(less) element	artist humor(less) person

Have students share their knowledge or use learner's dictionaries to form as many -*less* adjectives as possible with their group's nouns.

3. After steps 1 and 2, have groups write their nouns and adjectives on the board. Students complete the charts in their books using the information on the board.

NOUNS TO ADJECTIVES

Noun	+ Ending	= Adjective
sun	-y	sunny
luck		lucky
nerve		nervy
noise		noisy
sleep		sleepy
nation	-al	national
universe		universal
element		elemental
person		personal
child	-ish	childish
girl		girlish
boy		boyish
fool		foolish
danger	-ous	dangerous
mystery		mysterious
humor		humorous
moment		momentous
nerve		nervous
revolution	-ary	revolutionary
honor		honorary
element		elementary
moment		momentary
optimist	-ic	optimistic
class		classic
artist		artistic
base		basic

use	-less	useless
end		endless
base		baseless
count		countless
humor		humorless
limit		limitless
nerve		nerveless
noise		noiseless
power		powerless
sleep		sleepless
beauty	-ful	beautiful
wonder		wonderful
power		powerful
success		successful

Practice 6.1

All of the adjectives needed in this exercise are in the chart on pages 236–237 of the Student's Book.

Answers (Student's Book pages 237–238)

Interviewing My Classmate Loc

Loc Nguyen and I are in the same ESL class at Rancho Santiago College. At first I was (nerve) _____nervous_____ about interviewing him, although I knew that was (fool) _____foolish_____. In any case, his (boy) _____boyish_____ smile quickly made me feel comfortable. After I found out some (base) _____basic_____ information about Loc, he told me (count) _____countless_____ (humor) _____humorous_____ stories about his first few months in the U.S. For example, at first he worked three jobs and was always (sleep) _____sleepy_____. Once he went to the home of a new girlfriend for dinner—and fell asleep at the table! It was a (moment) _____momentary_____ nap, but it made a (power) _____powerful_____ impression on her parents. Later, I asked him more (person) _____personal_____ questions, such as how he likes the U.S. Loc said he feels (luck) _____lucky_____ to

be in this country. He feels the opportunities here are almost (limit) _____limitless_____.

Here he can pursue his (artist) _____artistic_____ interests. He is a dancer and hopes

to have a career in dance someday. Right now he is teaching dance in an after-school

program at an (element) _____elementary_____ school. I'm sure that Loc will be

(success) _____successful_____ in his future in this country, and I am glad that I had the

chance to interview him.

Writing Assignment 2

You might prepare students for the interview by having the class brainstorm some questions that could elicit interesting answers. Write the questions on the board for students to refer to while they are interviewing each other.

Grammar Point 7 Changing Verbs to Adjectives

EXPLORING THE GRAMMAR POINT

Additional examples (Student's Book page 238)

• Marta's house by the ocean is a **pleasant** place, and the sound of the waves **pleases** everyone who visits her.
• My mother **excels** at making jams and jellies. Her pies are also **excellent**.
• After a day in the garden, it isn't easy to **wash** all the dirt from your hands. It's a good idea to wear **washable** clothing too.

UNDERSTANDING THE GRAMMAR POINT

There is only one correct adjective for each verb in the word box. See Grammar Point 4 in this Teacher's Manual (page 153) for suggestions on using the chart.

Answers (Student's Book pages 238–239)

VERBS TO ADJECTIVES		
Verb	**+ Ending**	**= Adjective**
attract	-ive/-ative	attractive
conserve		conservative
effect		effective
talk		talkative

urge	-ant/-ent	urgent
repel		repellent
excel		excellent
please		pleasant
understand	-able	understandable
agree		agreeable
return		returnable
wash		washable

Practice 7.1

Most of the adjectives needed in this exercise are in the chart on pages 238–239 of the Student's Book.

Answers (Student's Book page 239)

Overly Talkative Salespeople

Salespeople are not always helpful when a person is trying to decide on a purchase. The other day I was shopping for a jacket, and I found an (attract)

_____attractive_____ one. I liked it because it was (conserve) _____conservative_____
        1   2

in color and style. It was also (wash) _____washable_____, and I travel a lot.
                                   3

Furthermore, the price was (excel) _____excellent_____ and it was (return)
                                   4

_____returnable_____ if I changed my mind. I decided to buy it.
                   5

Just then a salesperson came over to me. She was very (please)

_____pleasant_____, but she talked so fast that she wasn't (understand)
                  6

_____understandable_____. This almost made me change my mind about buying the jacket.
                  7

I asked her to let me think for a minute, and she was (agree) _____agreeable_____.
                                                      8

In the end, I decided for the second time to buy the jacket.

Grammar Point 8 ▸ -*ing* and -*ed* for Adjectives

EXPLORING THE GRAMMAR POINT

Answers (Student's Book page 240)

An Irish Legend

One day the king took his elder son with him on a long trip. After several hours, he said to his son, "Son, shorten the road for me." The son had no idea what to do, and the <u>disappointed</u> (king) turned around and returned home with his son.

Some time later, the king took his younger son on a trip and made the same request. Right away, the young man began to tell his father a long and <u>entertaining</u> (story). The (king) became so <u>interested</u> in the story that he never noticed the length of the journey.

Additional examples

- We went to a <u>boring</u> (movie). We were <u>bored</u>.
- It's <u>embarrassing</u> (to forget someone's name). (I) was <u>embarrassed</u> yesterday when I forgot your friend's name.
- My (son) is <u>interested</u> in astronomy and dinosaurs. He doesn't think (sports) are <u>interesting</u>.

UNDERSTANDING THE GRAMMAR POINT

Practice 8.1

Answers (Student's Book pages 240–241)

1. I flew to Canada. It took twenty-two hours. The flight was *(tiring)*/ *tired*.
2. I always get motion sickness, so I couldn't read during the flight. I was *boring* /*(bored)*.
3. It took two hours to go through Immigration. I was *exhausting* /*(exhausted)*.
4. When I arrived, my sister was waiting for me. The arrival was *(exciting)*/ *excited*.
5. At first everything was new and different. I was *fascinating* /*(fascinated)*.
6. Later, everything seemed strange and difficult. Living in Canada was *(frustrating)* / *frustrated*.
7. My English wasn't very good, and it was hard to go places and do things. I often felt *confusing* /*(confused)*.
8. Now things are easier, and I am getting used to my new life. I am feeling more *relaxing* /*(relaxed)*.

Practice 8.2

The task is open-ended and answers will vary.

You might have a few students do the exercise on the board while the others work in their books. Correct the sentences on the board. Then call on a few more students to read their sentences aloud, and ask the class for feedback.

EXPLORING THE GRAMMAR POINT

Additional examples (Student's Book page 242)

- We need a **summary** of your speech for the Web site. Could you **summarize** it for me?
- I don't know how to pronounce this word **correctly**. Could you tell me the **correct** pronunciation?

UNDERSTANDING THE GRAMMAR POINT

There is only one correct adverb or verb for each word in the box. See Grammar Point 4 in this Teacher's Manual (page 153) for suggestions on using the chart.

Answers (Student's Book page 242)

+ LY	
Adjective + -ly	**= Adverb**
careful	carefully
clear	clearly
correct	correctly
perfect	perfectly
slow	slowly

+ IZE	
Noun/Adjective + -ize	**= Verb**
emphasis	emphasize
real	realize
modern	modernize
summary	summarize

Practice 9.1

Answers (Student's Book page 243)

A Great Day

Last weekend I (priority) _____**prioritized**_____ my homework so that I had some
                                    1

time to relax on Sunday. I really enjoyed the time off. Then today, Monday, my ESL class

was especially satisfying. We handed in our writing assignments at the beginning of

class. I (real) _____**realized**_____ that some of the students were having problems
                        2

finishing the assignment. The instructor asked me to (summary) ____summarize____
3

my paper for the class, and I did. I (emphasis) ____emphasized____ my topic and
4

supporting ideas, and for once, I was (perfect) ____perfectly____ comfortable
5

in front of the class. Next, the instructor explained the new grammar lesson (slow)

____slowly____ and (clear) ____clearly____. I did the exercises
6   7

(careful) ____carefully____. (Final) ____Finally____, we had a quiz, and I
8   9

answered all the questions (correct) ____correctly____. What a great day!
10

Writing Assignment 3

There are two topics for students to choose from. One or the other should work for most students. If anyone feels unable to write about either topic, have them imagine having a garden and write about what that would be like.

Review Practice 14.1

Answers (Student's Book page 244)

1.   Part of Speech   Base Word

   a. attendance _____ noun _____   _____ attend _____

   b. heroic _____ adjective _____   _____ hero _____

   c. kissable _____ adjective _____   _____ kiss _____

   d. slowly _____ adverb _____   _____ slow _____

   e. sweetness _____ noun _____   _____ sweet _____

   f. theorize _____ verb _____   _____ theory _____

2. What is a present participle?   *The* -ing *form of a verb*
   For the sentences, answers will vary.

Review Practice 14.2

Answers (Student's Book page 245)

1. It's hard for me to be careful when I write. I am a _____ careless _____ writer.

2. It is very easy to love her. She is very _____ lovable _____.

3. Everyone felt encouraged by your words. Your words were _____ encouraging _____.

4. I noticed that he was kind. I noticed his _____ kindness _____.

5. Her voice was sweet. She sang _____ sweetly _____.

6. The job requires a driver's license. One _____ requirement _____ of the job is a driver's license.

7. He always looked at the world with humor. His view of the world was always _____ humorous _____.

8. They dance well. They are good _____ dancers _____.

9. He is able to accept difficulties in life. He is _____ accepting _____ of difficulties.

10. He was not allowed to be very active after his surgery. His _____ activity _____ was limited.

11. She enjoyed being active in local politics. She enjoyed her _____ activism _____.

12. We could not understand him. He was not _____ understandable _____.

Review Practice 14.3

Answers (Student's Book page 245)

Organization

~~Recent~~ **Recently** my teacher told me that my biggest problem in writing is organizing my ideas ~~effective~~ **effectively**. This was ~~surprised~~ **surprising** because I thought my biggest problem was grammar. However, this realization has been very ~~help~~ **helpful** for me. When I did my last writing ~~assign~~ **assignment**, I gave a lot of attention to ~~organize~~ **organization**. I was supposed to ~~reaction~~ **react** to a short magazine article. After the topic sentence, I ~~summarization~~ **summarized** the writer's main ideas briefly. Then I gave my own reactions to the article and ~~emphasis~~ **emphasized** my strongest point. In the ~~conclude~~ **conclusion**, I generalized about the ~~effective~~ **effect** the article may have had on others like me. I think it is my best ~~compose~~ **composition** so far. I am ~~pleasing~~ **pleased** with the results.

Review Practice 14.4

Answers (Student's Book page 246)

Dutch Elm Disease

A hundred years ago, most North American towns and cities were full of tall, ~~grace~~ **graceful** American elms. The trees lined both sides of ~~shade~~ **shaded / shady** streets. Even modest neighborhoods looked ~~welcome~~ **welcoming** because of their ~~beauty~~ **beautiful** elms.

Then, around 1930, the elms began to die of a new disease. The cause was a fungus that entered this country ~~accidental~~ **accidentally** from Europe. Beetles spread the fungus when they ~~colony~~ **colonize** the elms. The fungus ~~quick~~ **quickly** blocks the ~~disease~~ **diseased** trees' circulatory systems so that they cannot get water. Today, no American city has all its original elms, and most cities have none, or nearly none.

The disease is called Dutch elm disease because it ~~initial~~ **initially** arrived in elm wood from Holland. A few American elms are ~~natural~~ **naturally** able to ~~resistance~~ **resist** Dutch elm disease. Scientists are trying to ~~maximum~~ **maximize** this natural ~~resist~~ **resistance** through ~~select~~ **selective** breeding. Only time will tell if this strategy can save the American elm.

Final Do's and Don'ts

Say and Tell with Direct and Indirect Objects

ABOUT DIRECT AND INDIRECT OBJECTS

This section is a quick tutorial on direct and indirect objects, which are central to understanding the uses of *say* and *tell* discussed in this grammar point.

Additional examples (Student's Book page 248)

• We said **nothing**.
• He didn't tell **me his name**.
• They said **there was no problem**.
• She told **the police several different stories**.

EXPLORING THE GRAMMAR POINT

Answers (Student's Book page 248)

5. I said <u>that it was OK</u>.

6. He always says <u>he will take care of it</u>.

7. I told (John) that it was OK.

8. He always tells (me) <u>he will take care of it</u>.

UNDERSTANDING THE GRAMMAR POINT

Practice 1.1

Answers (Student's Book page 249)

1. My aunt once _____**told**_____ me that most problems exist only in our imaginations.

2. The guru _____**told**_____ his followers that people can change their lives by changing their attitude toward life.

3. Someone _____**said**_____ that laughter translates into any language, but jokes do not.

4. Graham Greene _____**said**_____ that in human relationships, kindness and lies are worth a thousand truths.

5. The speaker _____**told**_____ us that storms make trees grow stronger roots.

6. My accountant _____**told**_____ me that a fool and his money are soon parted.

7. Someone _____**said**_____ that when one teaches, two learn.

8. Thomas Edison _____**told**_____ somebody that he never did a day's work in his life. He _____**said**_____ it was all fun.

EXPLORING THE GRAMMAR POINT

Additional examples (Student's Book page 249)

- Lisa has a cat, but she just adopted **another** one.
  She wanted **another** cat to keep her old one company.
  She had an orange tabby, and then decided to get **another** just like it.

- Some governments are interested in **another**.

- Having **another** doesn't interest me.

UNDERSTANDING THE GRAMMAR POINT

The examples in the Student's Book (Exploring the Grammar Point, page 249) illustrate *another = a different*. The additional examples above illustrate *another = one additional*. The meanings are very similar and you may not wish to make a distinction for your students unless they ask.

Grammar Point 3 **Other** and **Others**

EXPLORING THE GRAMMAR POINT

Additional examples (Student's Book page 250)

- I just signed up for some classes at the YMCA. I took some **other** classes there last year.
- I took **others** at the Learning Annex, but I didn't like them as much.

UNDERSTANDING THE GRAMMAR POINT

Of course, the singular pronoun that pairs with *others* is *another*.

Practice 3.1

Answers (Student's Book page 251)

Careers in Photography

Many people have careers in photography. Some take pictures for movies. Some

run television cameras. ____Other____ people operate X-ray machines. Still
                            1

____others____ photograph weddings or ____other____ celebrations. There are
      2   3

many ____other____ jobs in photography besides taking pictures, though. One is
          4

developing film. ____Another____ is selling cameras and supplies. Camera repair is
                        5

____another____ related job. Many people also work in large manufacturing facilities
      6

that make photo paper, film, and ____other____ photographic supplies.
                                        7

EXPLORING THE GRAMMAR POINT

Additional examples (Student's Book page 251)

• Ellen has two cars. She loves her convertible, but she drives **the other car** to work.

  . . . she drives **the other one** to work.

  . . . she drives **the other** to work.

• I'm taking five classes this semester. One of them is on North Campus, and **the other classes** are on South Campus.

  . . . **the other ones** are on South Campus.

  . . . **the others** are on South Campus.

UNDERSTANDING THE GRAMMAR POINT

It is also common to use numbers with *the other*.

• . . . **the other four classes** are on South Campus.
• . . . **the other four** are on South Campus.

Practice 4.1

Answers (Student's Book page 252)

*Quiz: The Former Soviet Union**

1. Russia and Ukraine are the largest states of the former USSR.

   Can you name ___the others___?

2. Latvia and Lithuania are two of the three Baltic republics.

   Can you name ___the other___?

3. Lenin was the first leader of the USSR. Gorbachev was the last.

   How many of ___the others___ can you name?

4. St. Petersburg has had three names since it was founded by Peter the Great.

   One of ___the other___ names was Petrograd. Do you know ___the other___?

5. Eleven different seas border Russia. The Baltic Sea is one of them.

   Can you name ___the others___?

* The answers to this quiz are on Student's Book page 253.

EXPLORING THE GRAMMAR POINT

Additional examples (Student's Book page 252)

- **Correct:** The college is constructing two **new** buildings.
  Incorrect: two **news** buildings

- **Correct:** The new student **activity** center will have two **movie** theaters.
  Incorrect: student **activities** center . . . two **movies** theaters

Grammar Point 6 ▶ **Numerical Noun Adjectives**

EXPLORING THE GRAMMAR POINT

Additional examples (Student's Book page 253)

- **Correct:** My husband and I are short, but we have a **six-foot, five-inch** son.
  Incorrect: a **six-feet, five-inches** son

- **Correct:** We took a **two-week** vacation in August.
  Incorrect: a **two-weeks** vacation

UNDERSTANDING THE GRAMMAR POINT

Practice 6.1

Answers (Student's Book page 254)

1. First he had a _____twelve-month_____ training period. (of twelve months)

2. The management wanted to send him on a _____three-year_____ assignment to Egypt. (of three years)

3. They eventually sent him for a _____three-year_____ stay in East Africa. (for three years)

4. It was a _____two-week_____ journey to get there. (of two weeks)

5. He received a _fifteen-thousand-dollar_ salary. (of fifteen thousand dollars)

6. When he went to East Africa, he was a _____twenty-year-old_____ businessman. (twenty years old)

Practice 6.2

Answers (Student's Book page 254)

1. They have a _____two-story house_____ (house with two stories)
   near two _____golf courses_____ (courses for playing golf).

2. It's a _____four-bedroom house_____ (house with four bedrooms)
   on a _____three-acre lot_____ (lot of three acres).

3. The first floor has _____thirty-foot-high ceilings_____ (ceilings that are thirty feet high)
   and an _____eight-foot-wide fireplace_____ (fireplace that is eight feet wide).

4. There are many _____flower gardens_____ (gardens of flowers)
   and a big _____vegetable garden_____ (garden for growing vegetables).

5. There is also a separate _____guest house_____ (house for guests).

6. They have three cars and a _____three-car garage_____ (garage for three cars).

7. On the patio, there's a _____charcoal grill_____ (grill for cooking with charcoal), and a _____picnic table_____ (table for picnics).

Grammar Point 7 **Almost, Most (of), and Almost All**

EXPLORING THE GRAMMAR POINT

Additional examples (Student's Book page 255)

- **Incorrect:** **Almost** Dewey High School students want to go to college.
  Correct: **Most** Dewey High School students want to go to college.
  Correct: **Almost all** Dewey High School students want to go to college.

- **Incorrect:** **Almost** candy is bad for your teeth.
  Correct: **Most** candy is bad for your teeth.
  Correct: **Almost all** candy is bad for your teeth.

UNDERSTANDING THE GRAMMAR POINT

Additional examples (Student's Book page 255)

- **Most of my** high school classmates went to college.
- **Most of that** candy is bad for your teeth.

Practice 7.1

Answers will vary.

Suggested answers (Student's Book page 255)

1. _Almost all of my friends_ have cars.
   OR
   Most of my friends have cars.
2. _Most children_ like ice cream.
3. _Almost all Koreans_ eat *kim chi*.
4. _Most plants_ need sunshine to grow.
5. _Most students_ have homework to do.
6. _Most snow_ falls in winter.
7. _Almost all babies_ drink milk.
8. _Almost all cars_ cause pollution.

EXPLORING THE GRAMMAR POINT

Additional examples (Student's Book page 256)

• I get great benefits at work. I get **too many** vacation days. (not logical)
• Sometimes I have **too much** work, though.
• My boss asks me to take on **too many** projects at once.

UNDERSTANDING THE GRAMMAR POINT

Additional examples (Student's Book page 256)

• I get twenty vacation days a year. That's **a lot**.
• I can't finish my work in eight hours. There is **too much**, so I have to work late.
• We have six projects right now. That's **too many**.

Practice 8.1

Answers (Student's Book page 257)

1. There's a one-bedroom apartment near the school. The rent is $1400. That's
   _____*too much*_____ . *or* That's ___*a lot of money*___ .

2. A friend of mine is taking seven courses this semester. That's
   too many / a lot / too many courses / a lot of courses .

3. My physics textbook cost $75. That's
   too much / a lot / too much money / a lot of money .

4. A family in my town has twelve children. That's
   too many / a lot / too many children / a lot of children .

5. The cheapest ticket to the play is $44. That's
   too much / a lot / too much money / a lot of money .

6. Mr. Ogden has seventeen cats. That's
   too many / a lot / too many cats / a lot of cats .

7. I had to do six hours of homework last night. That's
   too many hours / too much homework / a lot / a lot of homework .

8. My nephew drinks about ten cans of soda a day. That's
   too many / too much soda / a lot / a lot of soda .

EXPLORING THE GRAMMAR POINT

Additional examples (Student's Book page 257)

• Patti went to bed **after** she did her homework.
• **After** Patti did her homework, she went to bed.
• Patti did her homework. **Afterwards**, she went to bed.

- Patti did her homework. She went to bed **afterwards**.
- Patti did her homework **after** she went to bed.

UNDERSTANDING THE GRAMMAR POINT
Additional examples (Student's Book pages 257–258)
- **Incorrect:** Patti did her homework, **after**, she went to bed.
- **Incorrect:** Patti did her homework. **After** she went to bed.

Practice 9.1
Answers will vary.

Suggested answers (Student's Book pages 258–259)
1. After I had dinner with a friend, I went home and went to bed early.
2. I worked for a few hours in the evening. Afterwards, I felt tired.
3. After I brushed my teeth, I went to bed. / I went to bed after I brushed my teeth.
4. I set the alarm clock for 7:00. Afterwards, I slept well.
5. After I decided to find out about my local community college, I visited the campus.
6. I filled out an application. Afterwards, I took the English and math placement tests.
7. After I spoke to a counselor, she helped me apply for financial aid.
8. I registered for classes. Afterwards, I went to my first class and bought my textbooks.

Grammar Point 10 *During* **and** *While*

EXPLORING THE GRAMMAR POINT
Additional examples (Student's Book page 259)
- Susan isn't eating very well **while** her husband is away.
  She usually surfs the Web **while** she eats.
- Sometimes she watches TV **during** dinner.
  She flips to other channels **during** the commercials.

Practice 10.1
Answers (Student's Book page 259)
1. Jesse watches the kids _____ while _____ his wife goes to her night class.
2. He fixes dinner _____ while _____ the kids watch TV.
3. Sometimes they all watch TV _____ during _____ dinner.
4. Usually, though, Jesse and the kids talk _____ while _____ they eat.
5. _____ During _____ most of the week, Jesse works overtime.
6. He's usually working _____ while _____ the kids and his wife are having dinner.
7. But on Tuesdays, _____ during _____ his wife's class, Jesse gets to know his children better.
8. Now he looks forward to Tuesday _____ during _____ the whole week.

EXPLORING THE GRAMMAR POINT

Additional examples (Student's Book page 260)

- **Sometimes** I dream of having a houseboat.
- I **sometimes** dream of having a houseboat.
- I dream of having a houseboat **sometimes**.
- **Sometime** I'd like to go on a boat trip.
- I'd like to go on a boat trip **sometime**.

UNDERSTANDING THE GRAMMAR POINT

Additional examples (Student's Book page 260)

- **Sometimes** I'm nervous about speaking in class.
- I am nervous **sometimes** about speaking in class.
- I am nervous about speaking in class **sometimes**.

Practice 11.1

Answers (Student's Book page 260)

1. I _____ sometimes _____ fall asleep in class.

2. _____ Sometime _____ I'll tell you about your Uncle Rob.

3. I hope I can see the Taj Mahal _____ sometime _____ .

4. _____ Sometimes _____ I don't know the answer.

5. I am _____ sometimes _____ late for class, but not often.

6. I forget what I'm doing _____ sometimes _____ .

7. _____ Sometime _____ I want to learn to play the piano.

8. I'd like to take my family to Ireland _____ sometime _____ .

UNDERSTANDING THE GRAMMAR POINT

Additional examples (Student's Book page 261)

- My godmother **is special** to me.
  She's a really **special person**.

- The party was a **specially planned** occasion.
  Yuki **invited** the Millers **specially**.

- I love to walk in the park, **especially on Sundays**.
  It's **especially nice** in spring.

Practice 12.1
Answers (Student's Book page 262)

Special Resource Center

El Camino College has a _____special_____ program to assist students with
$\underset{1}{}$

disabilities. The staff is _____specially_____ trained to help disabled students,
$\underset{2}{}$

_____especially_____ those with physical and learning disabilities, the deaf and
$\underset{3}{}$

hard of hearing, and the visually impaired. The center houses _____special_____
$\underset{4}{}$

equipment, such as large-print typewriters, talking computers, and reading machines.

The center's high-tech lab makes computers accessible to disabled students through

_____specially_____ designed equipment that helps students input, process, and
$\underset{5}{}$

output information. The curriculum includes _____special_____ classes in English,
$\underset{6}{}$

math, and career preparation. _____Especially_____ useful are the adaptive physical
$\underset{7}{}$

education classes, _____specially_____ created for disabled persons needing an
$\underset{8}{}$

individualized exercise program. All of these services are offered on a relatively small,

flat campus that has been _____specially_____ constructed to meet the needs of
$\underset{9}{}$

students with physical disabilities.

Grammar Point 13 ▸ *For Example*

UNDERSTANDING THE GRAMMAR POINT
Additional examples (Student's Book page 262)
- Some of my relatives love South Florida; **for example**, my brother, my cousin Javier, and two of my sisters.
- They usually find a way to go there once or twice a year. **For example**, Javier went there on business last month.
- **Incorrect:** All of my relatives love sports. For example tennis, water skiing, and deep-sea fishing.
  Correct: All of my relatives love sports. For example, Javier is a tennis fanatic, and my brother and sisters are into water skiing and deep-sea fishing.

Practice 13.1

Answers will vary.

Suggested answers (Student's Book page 263)

1. There are some good restaurants in my neighborhood <u>; for example, the Flea Market, Paprika, Esashi, and Madras Café.</u>

2. My friend loves to cook special dishes from our country <u>. For example, last Sunday he made chiles en nogada.</u>

3. It isn't easy to find ingredients for some dishes in American supermarkets <u>, for example, epazote.</u>

4. Sometimes my recipes don't work out <u>. For example, the last time I made pie crust, it was hard and greasy.</u>

5. I enjoy cooking together with friends <u>. For example, we sometimes get together at one person's house and everyone makes a different dish.</u>

6. Some of my favorite foods are not very good for you <u>, for example, French fries and doughnuts.</u>

7. When I'm at a good restaurant, I like to order something I would never make at home. <u>For example, I love good curry, but I'm too lazy to make it from scratch.</u>

8. When I travel, I like to try the local foods <u>; for example, soft-shell crabs in Maryland or jambalaya in Louisiana.</u>

Review Practice 15.1

Answers (Student's Book page 266)

1. If you want to mention the person you spoke to, which verb do you use: *say* or *tell*?   *Use tell to mention the person you spoke to. (Sentences will vary.) Mark told Andrew it was time to leave. Andrew told me he didn't want to go.*

2. Of the words and phrases below, which are adjectives and which are pronouns?   *Adjectives:*
   another, other, the other; Pronouns: another, the other, others, the others
   Of the pronouns, which are singular and which are plural?   *Singular: another, the other; Plural: others, the others*

3. If you have a car with four doors, how can you describe the car?   *It's a four-door car.*

4. Why is this sentence wrong? Correct it.
   Almost children like ice cream.
   It is wrong because almost *cannot modify a noun.*
   Corrected sentence: Almost all children like ice cream. or Most children like ice cream.

5. What is wrong with this statement? Correct it.
   The party was perfect. Too many people were there.
   The sentence is wrong because too many *expresses dissatisfaction. Since the party was perfect,* too many *is wrong.*
   Corrected statement: The party was perfect. A lot of people were there.

6. Why is the second sentence wrong? Correct it.
   He graduated from college last year. After, he got his first full-time job.
   The sentence is wrong because after *joins a dependent clause to an independent clause. It cannot introduce an independent clause.*
   Corrected sentence: He graduated from college last year. Afterwards, he got his first full-time job. or After he graduated from college last year, he got his first full-time job.

7. Which word begins a dependent clause: *during* or *while*?   *While introduces a dependent clause.*
   Write an example sentence.   *Example: I made the salad while Douglas set the table.*

8. Which word means *at an indefinite time in the future*: *sometime* or *sometimes*?   *Sometime means at an indefinite time in the future.*
   Write an example sentence.   *Example: I hope we'll meet again sometime.*

9. Circle the correct phrase in boldface type:
   She told **a special** / **a specially** / **an especially** good joke.

10. What is wrong with the following statement? Correct it.
    We read some difficult books in college. For example, *Remembrance of Things Past*, by Proust.
    This sentence is wrong because the phrase for example *must be (1) in the middle of a sentence, introducing a list, or (2) at the beginning of a complete sentence (an independent clause).*
    Corrected sentence: We read some difficult books in college, for example, Remembrance of Things Past, *by Proust. or We read some difficult books in college. For example, we read* Remembrance of Things Past, *by Proust.*

Review Practice 15.2

Answers (Student's Book page 267)

1. Sometimes I wonder if I will ever figure out what I want to do with my life. ~~Others~~ *Other*

   times, it doesn't seem like a problem.

2. My sister sent me some of her special cookies. She made them especially for me.

3. One reason is that it would be too expensive. ~~The other~~ *Another* reason is that it would take

   too much time. ~~Another~~ *The other* reason is that I don't want to. Those are my three reasons.

4. I ~~said~~ *told* them they were wrong. They said I was crazy.

5. ~~Most of~~ *Most* children like ice cream, but my ~~7-years-old~~ *7-year-old* brother is crazy about it~~, for~~

   ~~example,~~ *For example, he ate* a quart of Double Dutch Chocolate ice cream all by himself. ~~After~~ *Afterwards / After that,* he

   got sick.

6. Eloise always eats popcorn during the game. She ate two bowls of it during the last

   one. I never eat ~~during~~ *while* I'm watching TV, but I drank six cans of diet soda.

7. I keep the registration in the ~~gloves compartment~~ *glove compartment* of the car.

8. ~~Sometimes~~ *Sometime* while I'm in New York next month, I especially want to see the Statue of

   Liberty. I have already seen ~~almost~~ *most* of the ~~others~~ *other* sights.

9. Some people are afraid to take chances in life. ~~The others~~ *Others* take chances all the time.

   I am one of the others—somewhere in the middle.

10. There were too many people on the subway this morning. I could hardly breathe.

SECTION 5 REVIEW

REFRESHING YOUR MEMORY

Answers (Student's Book pages 268–269)

1. a. We live _____on_____ Lake Street.   Use *on* for streets.

   b. Put that _____on_____ the table, please.   Use *on* for surfaces.

   c. We met _____at_____ a dance.   Use *at* for events.

   d. Judy is _____at_____ work right now.   Use *at* for general locations.

   e. I was _____—_____ home all day.   The word *at* is not necessary.

   f. We moved here _____in_____ 2001.   Use *in* for periods of time.

   g. I'll see you _____on_____ Sunday.   Use *on* for days of the week.

2. a. It doesn't make any **difference** to me.
      This is an example of changing _____a verb_____ to _____a noun_____
      by adding _____-ence_____.

   b. It is hard to find job **security** these days.
      This is an example of changing _____an adjective_____ to _____a noun_____
      by adding _____-ity_____.

   c. The band is going to have a **national** tour.
      This is an example of changing _____a noun_____ to _____an adjective_____
      by adding _____-al_____.

   d. There is an **urgent** message for you.
      This is an example of changing _____a verb_____ to _____an adjective_____
      by adding _____-ent_____.

   e. He told one **boring** story after another.
      This is an example of using __a present participle__ as _____an adjective_____.

   f. She answered 82 percent of the questions **correctly**.
      This is an example of changing _____an adjective_____ to _____an adverb_____
      by adding _____-ly_____.

   g. He **emphasized** that it was important.
      This is an example of changing _____a noun_____ to _____a verb_____
      by adding _____-ize_____.

3. a. *other* and *the other*   *Other* is an adjective; *the other* is a singular pronoun.

   b. *too much* and *a lot*   *Too much* expresses dissatisfaction because the amount is large. *A lot* just says the amount is large.

   c. *during* and *while*   *During* introduces a prepositional phrase. *While* introduces a dependent clause.

   d. *say* and *tell*   *Say* takes only a direct object. *Tell* takes an indirect object + a direct object.

Section Review Practice 5.1
Answers (Student's Book page 269)

A Perfect Marriage

My older brother and his wife may have a perfect marriage. They met ~~on~~ *at* a high

school basketball game. Afterwards, *they* ~~were~~ were always together. They got married ~~in~~ *on* the

same day they graduated from high school. Some people said the marriage would never

last because they were too young. But ~~other~~ *others*, like me, said it would. ~~Afterwards~~ *After* high

school, they both went to college and got degrees in history. Now my brother teaches

high school history and June has a consulting business. Ron and June seem like they

were ~~special~~ *specially* made for each other. June loves Ron's kindness and ~~considerate~~ *consideration*. She also

admires his ~~limit~~ *limitless* patience with his students. Ron appreciates June's ~~optimist~~ *optimism* and her

~~humor~~ *humorous* attitude toward life. Neither of them is ~~perfectly~~ *perfect*, and they know it, but each of

them feels ~~accepting~~ *accepted* by ~~the others~~ *the other*.

There are some things they do to make their marriage work. The most ~~importance~~ *important*

thing they do is ~~priority~~ *prioritize* the marriage—nothing else comes first. ~~Other~~ *Another* thing is that they

spend ~~too much~~ *a lot* of their free time together, but they make sure they have time apart too.

They never go to bed mad, and they ~~say~~ *tell* each other "I love you" ~~on~~ every day. I hope

~~sometimes~~ *sometime* I will find a relationship as good as Ron and June's.

Answers (Student's Book page 270)

Two Heads Are Better Than One

"Two heads are better than one." This saying means that working together is more

~~effect~~ *effective* than working alone. I agree with this saying. ~~In~~ *At* work a few years ago, my boss

used a new network system to ~~connection~~ *connect* all the computers ~~on~~ *in* the office. After she

completed the ~~install~~ *installation*, some of the computers worked, but ~~other~~ *the others* did not. At first, my

boss tried to figure out what was wrong by herself. She worked ~~slow~~ *slowly* and ~~careful~~ *carefully*, but she

couldn't find the problem. Finally she ~~said~~ *told* me that she could not find it and asked me to

help her. When my boss showed me how she had connected the computers, I noticed

that the order of the steps was ~~incorrectly~~ *incorrect*. When I told her about my ~~discover~~ *discovery*, we both

made the necessary changes. ~~After,~~ *Afterwards,* all the computers ~~on~~ *in* the network worked ~~perfect~~ *perfectly*.

This experience showed me that ~~sometime~~ *sometimes* two people can solve a problem better than

one person working alone, ~~specially~~ *especially* if they ~~cooperation~~ *cooperate* well. It's important to ~~cooperative~~ *cooperate*

and work as a team so that more talents and skills can be applied in any situation.